A BEGINNERS GUIDE TO PANTOMIME

LAWRENCE WHYTE

POD edition

Typeset for print by Electric Reads
www.electricreads.com

Introduction

Every year hundreds of thousands of people in the United Kingdom take themselves off to a theatrical experience. Many of these people will not attend another visit to a theatre for the rest of the year. This peculiar form of behaviour usually occurs between the end of November and the beginning of April. The places they will flock to maybe major urban theatres, village and church halls, schools, workplaces or hospitals. The stars of the show might be television stars moonlighting onto the stage for only this part of the year, local amateur groups, church congregations, dance schools or family members.

The audience will be encouraged to do things that they would not usually be asked to do in traditional theatre shows. They will be encouraged to shout, cheer, boo, hiss, and even to get up on stage to take part in the show. Most of them will do this willingly and will have come to the show to actively participate. In short they will be watching or performing in the peculiar theatrical performance of Pantomime. Oh yes they will!

The idea of writing the book emerged during a

conversation with an American friend of mine. We were talking about our interests and I mentioned that I had taken part in a number of Pantomimes. He had no idea of what a Pantomime was and as I tried to explain it became more complicated. How do you try to help someone make sense of a show in which the Principle Boy is played by a girl and one of the leading ladies is dressed elaborately as a woman!

Later another friend came to see me in his first panto and was left feeling bewildered and confused by the whole event. He too had never heard of Pantomime and struggled to get to grips with some of the 'saucy' scenes on stage. It made me realise that there might be other people who might not have had the experience of the Pantomime so an introductory text might be a useful contribution to their understanding and a means by which the discomfort my friend went through might be reduced.

The aim of the book is to introduce the novice Pantomime audience member or budding thespian into the peculiarities of this magical theatrical style. Going to the theatre is such a wonderful experience and for many young people the traditional Pantomime is their first introduction into this world. For theatre goers who have been used to more conventional dramatic shows, exposure to the Pantomime might become an overwhelming experience. This short book is an introduction to the traditional Christmas show and I hope that it will be an enjoyable and informative read.

This book will examine the extraordinary world of Pantomime. The first chapter will explore the history and origins of this eccentric form of performance art. The second chapter will outline the storylines of the top 10 Pantomimes performed in the UK. The next four chapters will summarise the main character types found in most Pantomimes; the Principal Boy, the Dame, the Villain and the Good Fairy. The careers and backgrounds of 10 actors and actresses who have played the particular part will be outlined to highlight how the role can be played differently. Chapter Seven will suggest how you as an audience member might behave at a Pantomime performance by introducing you to the rules and obligations of the audience member.

Chapter One
The History of Pantomime

Any analysis of the world of Pantomime should start with an examination of its origins. Pantomime, or Panto, emerged as a form of musical comedy stage production in Ancient Greece. The Greek word 'Pantomime' broadly translated as 'imitating all' was a respected form of entertainment with a strong emphasis on dancing and movement and encompassed both tales of tragedy and comedy. It does however seem to be more sexual and erotic than the contemporary Pantomime performed nowadays which is specifically aimed at families and children.

The Pantomime spread to the Roman Empire as a form of popular entertainment. But it was eventually banned by the Catholic Church on the grounds of its alleged innuendo about sexual behaviour. Sadly little evidence survived from either the Greek or Roman times which might give us a greater insight into the subject matter or stories on which the Pantomimes were based. It could be assumed that it was in some cases a controversial or subversive form of public display in these periods but highly popular among the audience. Whether or not the shows invited public participation is unknown but the combination of music, songs, dance, mime and comedy can be perceived as precursor to the ways in which contemporary Pantomime emerged. The influence of the Catholic Church as a censor to the public display of this form of entertainment suggests a subversive content to shows would not be uncommon.

Following the Roman period the history of Pantomime seems to be relatively unknown or undiscovered. However the development of the modern Pantomime can be traced to four influencing factors; the Mummers Plays of the Middle Ages, the Italian Commedia dell'arte, the Victorian Variety theatre and the growth of the mass media and celebrity status. One of the important features of the Pantomime is its capacity to evolve and change and to take on new forms in response to historical and social factors.

In the Middle Ages the Mummers Plays were traditional English folk plays performed during the festive seasons when rural communities came together to celebrate and attend markets and entertainment events. The performances contained many of the archetypal elements of the contemporary Pantomime including stage frights, coarse humour, gender reversal of roles and fantastic mythical creatures.

Mummers Plays were performed by amateur actors known as mummers or guisers. Sadly no scripts or performance details survive from this era so it is difficult to fully elaborate upon plots and storylines. But the word 'mummer' is said to derive from the middle English 'mum' (silent) or Greek 'mommo' (mask) but is more likely to be associated with early new high German 'mummen' (distinguished person').

Although broadly comic in tone, the plays seem to be based on underlying themes of duality and resurrection and underpinned by a battle between two or more characters representing 'Good' versus 'Evil'. Often the plays included a magic potion which is able to resuscitate a slain character and the plays may have been used to sell and market the potion to the general public.

The principle characters in the Mummers play are the hero, his chief opponent (the Villain), the Fool and a Quasi-Medical man or Shaman. The defining feature of the performance is the opportunity for the quasi-medical man to bring back to life the hero or the Villain through the use of the magic potion. Whilst several varieties of the play were thought to exist it was not unusual for the hero to be St George and the Villain a Turkish knight or foreign soldier. Given that few of the audience would have seen someone of foreign extraction, the guise of the Villain could be exaggerated to make them seem grotesque and evil.

A major reason for the use of disguise in the plays was to minimise the stigma of begging. Performers did not want to be perceived as begging from the general public and the play could be used as a means of raising extra money for the festive season for low paid workers. The activity of 'mumming' seems to have peaked at the end of the 19th century. The plays generally died out by the onset of the First World War although variations of it can still be seen in the revivals of songs and dances in rural locations.

Mummers' plays were formerly performed throughout much of the English speaking world. There are a few surviving traditional remnants of Mummers associated with Morris and sword dancing groups. The characters might be introduced through a series of short speeches usually in rhyming couplets so they may present themselves in the course of the play's action. The Villain character would normally be the one who is sent to extract money from the audience.

Mummers' plays were not only popular in the UK but had widespread appeal internationally with similar theatrical experiences being reported in Ireland, Germany, the USA and Austria. Although the heroes and Villain might be different in these countries, the general themes of 'Good' versus 'Evil' and the abundant use of songs and local dances would have remained the same. Luckily some of the original scripts from the 19th century have been discovered giving a much less speculative idea of what the mummers plays were like.

The second major influence on the evolution of the modern Pantomime was the Commedia dell'arte. This was a form of theatre characterised by masked 'types' which began in Italy in the 16th century. The closest translation of the name is 'comedy of craft of improvisation' and consisted of a series of sketches. This form of theatre became the first entirely professional theatre allowing actors and actresses the luxury of developing this craft and using more imaginary ways to develop their acting skills.

Performances took place on outdoor, temporary stages

and relied on various props in place of extensive scenery. Often theatre groups could seek patronage from rich people or local towns in which they played. Extra funding could be gained by donations by passing the hat so that the audience could watch the performance free of charge.

The characters of the Commedia dell'arte usually represented fixed social types such as foolish old men, devious servants or military officers full of bravado. The characters often started off as satirised stereotypes and became the archetypes of many of the favourite characters of the 17th and 18th century European theatre. The first recorded Comedia dell'arte was recorded in 1551. It was a form of theatre which contrasted with the more formal Commedia erudita which had written scripts and little room for improvisation. The ability to fund the dell'arte troupe meant that the conditions for stabilising performance could be sustained.

In Commedia dell'arte female roles were played by females which gave much needed respect to female performers in Europe. Sadly it would take much longer for such respectability to be achieved in the UK. But there was still some resistance to the idea of females performing in Europe and there were moves to get them banned in the 1570s. By the early 17th century the Commedies were moving away from pure improvisation to specific and delineated acts and characters. As the genre moved into more rural locations, it evolved towards a more Pantomime style. The form of Commedia dell'arte also began to spread more widespread geographically, particularly in France.

Each country developed the genre into more localised forms. For example Pantomime partially owes its evolution to the characters types of the Commedia dell'arte particularly Harlequin. The Harlequin is based on a mischievous demon character in popular French passion plays. The first known appearance of the Harlequin on stage is thought to be 1262. The character metamorphosed into a 'zany' persona in the Commedia dell'arte. It was adopted into the Pantomime and over time the character became the 'King of Pantomime' featuring as a magical character that danced, mimed and did acrobatics. For over 150 years Harlequin dominated the Pantomime as the main character.

Conventional plot lines were written on themes of jealousy, sex, love and aging. Not all sketches were comic as the genre embraced drama and tragedy. Performances made use of well-rehearsed jokes and stock physical gags as well as on the spot improvised routines involving slapstick. Since at least some of the productions were improvised, dialogue and action could be easily changed to satirise bad scandals and current events, whilst still retaining the old jokes and routines. Characters were identified by costumes, masks and props and like the Harlequin, many of the characters contained the antecedents of modern clowning.

The classic plot involved two of the characters falling in love. But they were prevented from their desires to get married by one or several of the other characters. This leads the lovers to seek the help of the servants to help them realise their ambitions. Typically the story would end happily with the marriage of the lovers and forgiveness of those who initially stood in their way. Of course music and dance were central to the performances and were highly prized skills amongst the theatrical community.

The third major influence on the development of Pantomime was the Victorian Music Hall tradition. By the time of the Victorian era, Pantomime had evolved into more or less the performances of contemporary times. The Harlequinades had ceased to be a part of the shows and were replaced by traditional stories such as 'Jack and the Beanstalk' and 'Cinderella. Adaptations of the classic fairy tales into a Pantomime form included the use of puns and word plays which have become a standard in all Pantomimes.

Performances were also longer with some Pantomimes stretching out for the whole evening and lasting five hours. Improved technology meant better lighting, more elaborate costumes and spectacular scene changes. The Drury Lane Theatre became the centre of the most spectacular shows with huge casts and performing animals.

The stock characters of the Principal Boy and the Dame became the main players and several musical actors and actresses, such as Marie Lloyd and Dan Leno, were invited to play these roles. It became a tradition for the Pantomime to open on Boxing Day and to become associated with the festive season of Christmas. In doing so the shows began to be strongly associated with children and families and were adapted so that some of the humour could be hidden behind innuendo to keep adults entertained as well.

Christmas Pantomimes often included children in their

casts and the Drury Lane Theatre included children's ballet or dancing. The children were drawn from working class backgrounds and were expected to be disciplined and to work hard. The Victorian Pantomimes incorporated all kinds of magical scenes and special effects. This required major advances in the sets and scenery with the introduction of elaborately hinged flaps, pivots and slots, flying machinery and painted canvas cloths. Particular favourites were the secret chamber in the sets or underfloor trap-doors which could make transformational scenes appear like a piece of magic.

Scene changes and traps were co-ordinated by large groups of stage hands and the more elaborate sets might require 50 or 60 stage hands. Some of the larger theatres had enormous water tanks so that waterfalls and fountains could be created on stage. Gas lighting was introduced on to the London stage in 1817 replacing the candlelight which had provided illumination before. In 1881 electric lighting was used in the Pantomime production at the Savoy Theatre, London.

But the development of the Pantomime could not have evolved without the diversity and skills of the Victorian Music Hall performer. So much of what was successful in the Music Halls was transported into the Christmas Pantomime and the big stars of stage were invited to perform their songs and dances during the festive period.

Stars of the time could make their name with only one or two famous songs. The songs were about day to day life and the lyrics reflected the hardship and austerity of the times with content being about bailiffs, the mother-in-law, henpecked husbands, drink and debt. Other songs were romantic, sentimental and patriotic and could be included or adapted to fit the Pantomime stories. Audiences would return for repeat performances to hear the same jokes and songs because they were associated with favourite actors and actresses. Many of the great Music Hall performers such as Dan Leno, Marie Lloyd, Gus Elen and George Robey went on to perform in Pantomimes.

But it is not just singers who would make their mark in Victorian Pantomime. Female impersonators like Malcolm Scott had made his name as a straight actor but turned his hand to specialise in playing women and he led the way for more performers to take up the art of impersonation. Of course their abilities and comic turns were natural conditions to playing the Dame in the Pantomime.

Speciality acts such as dancers, acrobats, magicians and aerial acts would also provide performers who could adapt their specialised skills and make the move from Music Hall to Pantomime. For example, jugglers, cyclists, sword swallowers and animal acts were to find a natural home in the Christmas show adding to the spectacle and glamour of the Pantomime. Given that the locations for most of the traditional stories were in idyllic or faraway lands the opportunities to incorporate specialist acts into stories were numerous.

By the twentieth century the structure and content of the modern Pantomime was generally in place. The storylines represented the adaptation of the classic fairy tales. The scenery and the sets had become more technologically advanced allowing for the transformation and magical routines to be seamlessly enacted to the delight and wonder of the audience. The diversity was established with a wide variety of specialist acts complementing the comic routines, dancing and singing of the show. Finally the family orientated traditions of the Pantomime had been established and the show became a regular part of their Christmas experience.

But Pantomime was under threat from other forms of entertainment. Cinema, radio, television and later DVDs and video games were part of the mass entertainment industry which were all competing for the attention of audiences and Pantomime was in danger of being squeezed out. Indeed by the 1950s and 1960s the idea of Pantomime was being seen as old fashioned and not suited to the needs of the modern audience. Pantomime needed to be rescued and ironically the saviour of the show came from the very source of the threat to its existence, the celebrity!

The modern Pantomime was liberated by the employment of the mass media celebrity from show business and sport. So the final major influence on the evolution of the Pantomime was the growth of its celebrity base. The idea of using guest stars was new to the modern era. In the 19th century the Drury Theatre in London, in particular, hired well-known variety artists for their performances.

But the number of celebrities now employed in the Pantomime world has grown immensely in the present day. Pop stars, reality television stars, sportsmen and women, weathermen and weatherwomen and Uncle Tom Cobley and all are now appearing in a Pantomime near you this Christmas. And celebrities are responsible for bringing audiences back through the theatre doors and giving children their first theatre experience.

Celebrities are attracted to Pantomime for several reasons. First it is lucrative and the season is relatively short so it can be planned into busy filming and theatre schedules. Second it can revive a flagging career if you have not been so visible on stage and screen in other productions. Third it is novel with the American stars in particular having no other genre to compare it with from their own theatre tradition. Fourth it is fun and many stars who have been reluctant to consider Pantomime have found that it becomes a truly wonderful theatrical experience.

Even one of the greatest actors of modern times, Sir Ian Mckellen, donned a plethora of bizarre and outrageous costumes to play the role of Widow Twanky. He was very clear about his motivation for doing so as well by stating that it's 'got everything theatrical; song, dance, verse, slapstick, soliloquy, audience participation, spectacle, cross-dressing and a good plot'.

But possibly the biggest motivation for celebrities committing to Pantomime is the audience interaction. It remains the last bastion of the Music Hall variety show so you can litter the show with gags and routines and get a fantastic reaction. As one notable actor commented 'you don't get that with Shakespeare'. In Pantomime anything goes!

Celebrated celebrities to appear in Pantomime are too numerous to mention but some deserve their names to be spot-lighted. For example the pop singer Cliff Richard appeared in the Pantomime 'Aladdin' alongside his backing group, The Shadows, who played; Wishee, Washee, Noshee and Poshee! Similarly after 44 professional fights and 15 years in the professional boxing ring, Frank Bruno put himself on the stage to play a variety of roles in Pantomimes up and down the country to prolong his career and became an instant hit by his capacity to send himself up and not take himself too seriously.

Pantomime, as has been explained, has evolved over time and has been subject to a number of influences to become this unique British institution which people not raised in its traditions have difficult in understanding or appreciating. To the outsider it looks a mish-mash of different theatrical genres performed by a group of actors and actresses hamming it up on stage. But to the seasoned observer the subtle actions of the actors and actresses and the nuances of the show's storylines are presented in a chaotically sophisticated way that takes weeks and months to perfect.

Chapter Two
The Top Ten Pantomimes

The Pantomime story is basically a battle of 'good' against 'evil'. No matter if the story is set in medieval England, ancient China, exotic Egypt or fantasy land, the overall moral of the story is that 'Good' will triumph over 'Evil'. However in order to reach the outcome which the Pantomime requires there are a stock list of characters who play out the story and are either on the side of 'good' or 'evil'. Their names, occupations, social backgrounds and social classes might change but the essential intention of the character stays the same.

Where to begin? Listed below are the ten most popular Pantomimes. The shows which are likely to be playing at a theatre or church hall near you and which attract the biggest audiences. They are listed in no particular chronological order and a brief storyline is included for each one.

Cinderella: Before the days of robust child protection policies, here is a Pantomime story dealing with issues of child neglect and cruelty. For those who wish to delve deeper into the psychological roots of ancient tales, the Pantomime is also encased within a contemporary framework of family re-configuration and the stereotype of the wicked step-mother and emotionally absent father. It could have been written by Freud but it wasn't!

This is the classic 'rags to riches' storyline which is represented in many countries from Scandinavia to Romania. The first stage appearance of the story in England was at the Theatre Royal, Drury Lane in 1804 so there is no doubt it is a 'stayer'. Although the Pantomime script was written anonymously it was based on a fairy tale by the French writer Perrault.

A wealthy widower has remarried a vain and selfish woman who has strong interests in money and status. You might like to call her a gold-digger! She has two daughters by a previous relationship, parentage on the fathers side unspecified, who are equally as vain and selfish as their mother is. The major difference is that the mother is a 'looker' whilst her daughters are not. The widower, who may have been still grieving his first wife, when he married again, is not the brightest button on the coat. But he has been blessed with a beautiful young daughter who is a girl of virtue, purity and goodness. The scene is set for an emotional roller-coaster ride.

The wicked stepmother and her two daughters coerce the widower's daughter into a life of servitude. The poor girl has to work all hours of the day and night doing menial chores around the house and pander to the demands of her step siblings. After she has completed all the chores for the day, she retires to a cold room and curls up near to the fire in an effort to stay warm. Usually in the morning she finds herself covered in cinders which give the step-sisters the opportunity to christen her 'Cinderella'. This situation continues for a long time without the knowledge of her loving father who is dominated by his second wife. However with fortitude and good grace Cinderella continues to graft hard with little reward but with a resilient attitude that things can only get better!

One day, the handsome Prince of the Kingdom invites all the young ladies in the land to a grand 'Ball'. He is planning to choose a wife from amongst the ladies and to settle down to a life lived happily ever after. Much fuss and planning takes place in the widower's household as the two step-sisters set about choosing their wardrobes for the 'Ball'. They take great pleasure in taunting Cinderella by telling her that servants are not invited to the 'Ball'. Despite oodles of make-up and a lot of the widower's money being spent on expensive gowns, the step-sisters would still have difficulty in being featured highly on the Kingdom's top 100 most desirable females!

Sickened by sadness and despair, Cinderella breaks down in tears when her step-sisters depart for the 'Ball'. However with a glimmer of magic, her Fairy Godmother appears and begins the process of transforming Cinderella from menial house servant to a beautiful young lady. Think 60 minute make-over with Claire Sweeney as the Fairy Godmother!

Using her trusty magic wand, the Fairy Godmother is able to change mice into horses, a rat into a coachman and Cinderella's rags into a beautiful jewelled gown. Please note that no animals are harmed during this transformation process. To complete the outfit Cinderella is given a pair of delicate glass slippers which do not seem to have caught on as a fashion line.

However like everything in life there are always conditions, so Cinderella please read the small print. Clause one shows that our charming young debutante may only go to the Ball if she promises to leave the venue at mid-night. Failure to do so will result in the spell being broken and the transformation being reversed.

At the Ball the entire court is entranced by Cinderella, the mysterious beauty who has appeared out of nowhere. Particularly smitten is the Prince who thinks she is a bit of alright and wants to get better acquainted with her. We have to assume his intentions are honourable! They dance, they stare into each other's eyes, they hold each other close and they whisper sweet nothings in each other's ears. All of this is watched by the wicked step-mother and the step-sisters who are consumed with jealousy but are oblivious as to who their rival, for the Prince's hand, is.

Just before mid-night Cinderella remembers the curfew and when the clock strikes, she flees from the Palace to get back home before she is exposed as just a poor servant girl. But because she is in such a hurry she leaves behind a glass slipper. The Prince chases after her and although she is too quick for him, he manages to find the glass slipper and vows to his trusted friend, Dandini, to find the beauty who has evaded him and to make her his wife.

The Prince embarks on an endless journey around the

Kingdom in search of the beautiful girl. The organisation and administration of the search is carried out by Dandini because in the order of things royalty does not do the practical things. At each place where there were girls the Prince orders each of them to put on the glass slipper because he knows that if the shoe fits then he has got his girl. But the search is fruitless and they eventually arrive at the widower's house and begin the process of shoe fitting.

Of course the step–sisters are keen to be measured but alas and alack the shoe does not fit either of them. Sensing that there may be other girls in the house the Prince finds Cinderella (or alternatively in modern tales Cinderella asserts her authority) and she gets to try on the slipper. Lo and behold the slipper fits and it proves that Cinderella is the mysterious beauty who the Prince has been looking for. Oh what joy as the finale takes place back at the Palace where the wedding of the Prince and Cinderella takes place before an excited crowd. True to her nature Cinderella forgives her step-mother and step-sisters and everyone lives happily ever after!

This is all great and classic Pantomime material with lots of opportunities for glamourous costumes, gallant behaviour, audience participation and magical transformations which will appeal to audiences of all ages and it is easy to see why Cinderella is so popular with panto crowds. It is timeless and enchanting to watch.

There is no Dame part in Cinderella as the two step-sisters play this part between them. The character of Buttons, a friend of Cinderella interacts with the step-sisters to create a comic team. He tells lots of jokes to keep the audience amused or to cheer up the mistreated Cinderella. Often these jokes are insults directed at the two ugly sisters, either to their face or behind their backs. Buttons harbours a secret love for Cinderella but is happy for her when she finds love in the arms of the handsome Prince.

Aladdin: Modern productions shorten the title of this Pantomime from its full appellation of 'Aladdin and his Magic Lamp'. Its origins are from the classic tales of the Arabian Nights. This is a story which supports the proposition that ambition and aspiration will get you to where you want to be. It's a 'rags to riches' tale which is based on guile and the ability to spot an opportunity rather relying on physical attribution of beauty like Cinderella. The Pantomime was first performed in 1788. Strangely the action takes place between a mixture of Chinese and Arabic settings. By the time the story of Aladdin had got established as a Pantomime the characters and location of the original Arabian Nights story had changed dramatically. The main location switched from Baghdad to Peking and Aladdin's mother, Widow Twanky, became a washerwoman who runs the local laundry.

Aladdin is an impoverished young man growing up in Peking who is on a slippery slope towards delinquency until salvation sets in. His mother works hard trying to make money out of doing other people's laundry and tries to provide a stable and loving home for her two sons; Aladdin and Wishy-Washy. But money is hard to come by and Aladdin sets out to spot opportunities to earn some cash and realise his entrepreneurial ambitions.

A chance meeting with the Emperor's daughter, the Princess, who lives at the local Palace results in Aladdin being affected by Cupid's little arrow and falling head over heels in love. He is well and truly smitten and daydreams about ways in which he can become better acquainted with her. Of course these involve having cash and status which the Princess and the Emperor will equate with someone of importance that the Princess can socialise with.

As luck would have it he is recruited by a visiting Sorcerer who promises him substantial rewards if the boy will work for him to retrieve an oil-lamp from a booby-trapped cave. Aladdin becomes trapped in the cave when he refuses to give the Sorcerer the oil-lamp. He has become curious about its value. He inadvertently rubs the lamp and is astonished to conjure up a 'genie' who will obey his commands because he has set him free.

Of course Aladdin wants to be out of the cave as an initial wish and then become a man of wealth and privilege. The genie grants these wishes as this is his function in life and soon Aladdin has renewed his acquaintance with the Princess. Naturally he is received with open arms by the emperor who is experiencing a fiscal crisis of his own in a time of marked austerity. Everything is set fair for the lad until the evil Sorcerer somehow manages to steal the magic lamp and bring the genie under his control and further his quest for world-wide domination.

But he has not taken into consideration Aladdin's intelligence and ability to retrieve the situation. Somehow they all end up in an Arabic Country, usually Egypt, and Aladdin's plan to capture the lamp is put into operation. The finale is a battle between our resourceful hero and the evil Sorcerer which results in Aladdin getting the lamp back, punishing the Sorcerer, getting re-united with the Princess, rewarding his mother and finding contentment in a life of wealth. That sounds like a pretty good life-plan!

Widow Twanky is generally recognised as one of the great Dames in Pantomime mythology. She first appears in 1861 and, although not integral to the plot, is the source of interaction with the audience through jokes and innuendo. A classic scene revolves around items of laundry on her washing line. The name 'Twankey' comes from a cheap blend of Chinese tea which has an inferior grade of green tea with an old, ragged, open leaf. The implication being that the Widow is 'past her best'.

The comic duo is generally a pair of policemen who are sent to arrest the errant boy but fail spectacularly. They engage in a fair amount of banter with the audience making this one of the most interactive of all the Pantomimes. When you combine the comic antics of the policemen, Widow Twanky and Wishy Washy, there are plenty of laughs to be had in this show!

The Pantomime is full of opportunities for set builders to be inventive with scenes set if China, the cave and Arabia. There are plenty of thrills and room for spectacular fight scenes as well as romantic interludes. You can understand why it is a firm favourite with Pantomime audiences.

Dick Whittington: This is a Pantomime based on a real

life character rather than a fairy tale or a legend. Richard (Dick) Whittington was born around 1350 and really did become the Lord Mayor of London in 1397, 1406 and 1419, which is a more notable achievement than either Ken Livingstone or Boris Johnson, and they do not have a Pantomime written about them. Some might say they were a Pantomime but I will not get drawn on political arguments!

Whittington was a successful merchant and came from a wealthy family in Gloucestershire. However from a Pantomime perspective he was a penniless boy who set off to make his fortune in the big city of London. It is a story of a poor person making good through doing good for others. Through hard work and benevolence he rises through society to reach a position beyond his wildest dreams. The Pantomime first appears in 1814 and has become an established part of the festive season.

Of course in the Pantomime version of this true story, several characters have been added to embellish Dick's climb to the top. Most notably these are; his Cat, the Dame, the Fairy and the Demon of the Bells. Interestingly the Villain of the piece is King Rat and this is a reference to the fear of these creatures as carriers of the plague. Hence the Cat, who is a traditional predator of rats, is portrayed as protective and clean. Europe was affected by the Black Death pandemic which peaked in 1346-53 and was responsible for approximately 70 – 200 million deaths in the middle ages. Further pandemics continued to occur and significantly the Great Plague of London in 1665 to 1666 resulted in the deaths of 100,000 people or a quarter of its population.

The spread of the plague was attributed to infected vermin including rats so that the fear of mortality from the plague was tangible and the use of the rat as a Villain is entirely understandable in the context of the location of London as the setting for the Pantomime.

Dick is told that the streets of London are 'paved with gold' and so he sets off to make his fortune. He arrives in the City penniless and without a friend. But he soon meets Tommy the Cat who becomes his friend, companion and good luck charm. The two chums bump into Alice Fitzwarren, the daughter of Alderman Fitzwarren, a prominent figure in London.

Alice offers Dick and Tommy work in their shop. Soon the couple, Alice and Dick, fall in love and it is not long before Dick has gained the trust of the Alderman. He and Tommy are given the job of guarding the shop's safe overnight with all the takings in it. However the dastardly King Rat steals the money and 'in order to disgrace Dick, places it in the boy's pocket. When the Alderman demands that all staff be searched, the money if found in Dick's possession.

Shunned by his new friends and in disgrace, Dick and Tommy decide to go back to Gloucestershire. But on Highgate Hills, he hears the bells of London calling him by ringing 'Turn Again Whittington'. He is told he will become Lord Mayor of London, not once, not twice but three times! Buoyed by the messages they have received the pair turn around and start to walk back to London.

The scene moves to the docks of London. The Alderman has a ship which is setting off on a voyage on the first tide.

Dick and Tommy stow away but King Rat also hitches a ride with several of his henchman. The ship is wrecked and the stowaways are washed ashore in a foreign land. The rats have also made it ashore and have taken refuge in the Sultan's Palace causing mayhem. The Sultan offers a reward to anyone who can rid his Palace of the vermin. The reward is a substantial amount of money.

Enter Tommy the Cat, a creature never before seen in this foreign land. Together with his friend Dick, they vanquished King Rat and his followers from the Palace. With his new found wealth Dick is able to return to London, marry his true love Alice and rise to become the Lord Mayor of London. Everyone live happily ever after and Dick becomes a famous predecessor to Boris and Ken!

The Dame in this Pantomime is Sarah the Cook. She works for Alderman Fitzwarren and has a helper called Idle Jack. There is a classic baking scene between Sarah, Jack and often the Alderman, which causes pandemonium on stage and a great deal of mess. But it is very well received by the kids in the audience who delight in the bags of flour and sugar being distributed around the kitchen. They both somehow make the journey to the foreign land and gets involved in the banishing of King Rat. Given Sarah and Idle Jack are such strong characters, they usually double up as a comic duo.

Peter Pan: Some might argue that 'Peter Pan' is not strictly a Pantomime in the traditional sense and more of a theatrical musical. But who cares if it makes no reference to Christmas as it is still a story which delights audiences when performed at the Yuletide time of year. It is a tale of a mischievous boy who can fly and who never grows up. Peter Pan is a dark tale of the value of families, the innocence of childhood and how our self-identity is shaped by our past and present experiences of life. It is a story which soars to great heights of excitement and poignant moments of sadness and reflection on the choices we have in life. If this sounds a little bit existential, then I apologise for when children see the Pantomime 'Peter Pan' they do not get as hung up on the psychological messages supposedly contained within the tale. They just delight at the spectacle of it all!

Peter lives in Neverland, a mystical place in which he can indulge in exciting adventures. But at night he calls on the Darling family home in Bloomsbury where he listens to Mrs Darling's bedtime stories by the open window. You have to accept this was before television and video games! One night Peter is spotted and, whilst trying to escape, he leaves his shadow behind. On returning to collect it, Peter wakes Mrs Darling's daughter, Wendy. She succeeds in re-attaching his shadow to his body and Peter learns that she too knows a lot of bedtime stories. He invites Wendy to Neverland to be a mother figure to his gang, the 'Lost Boys'. These are children who have fallen out of their prams when their nurses were looking the other way. If they are not claimed within seven days, they are sent to Neverland. There are no 'Lost Girls' as girls are thought to be too clever to fall out of their prams.

Wendy agrees to go with Peter to Neverland but wishes to take her younger brothers John and Michael with her. The inhabitants of Neverland build a house for Wendy (hence the Wendy House) and her brothers begin to adopt the behaviours of the 'Lost Boys'. Wendy takes care of the boys who have lacked a feminine touch in their lives and regales them with bedtime stories. Peter is obviously the leader and he leads the gang into lots of adventures.

On one of these adventures Peter saves Tiger-Lily, a Native American, from an imminent pirate attack. The Leader of the pirates is the evil Captain Hook who blames Peter for the loss of his arm after being bitten by a crocodile. As an act of revenge Captain Hook kidnaps Wendy and her brothers and tries to kill Peter by poisoning him. But his friend, Tinker Bell the fairy, drinks the poison herself and nearly dies.

Peter goes to find Hook and rescue Wendy. He has a fierce duel with Captain Hook and forces the Villain off the ship and into the jaws of the waiting crocodile who has been stalking Hook after taking a fancy to the taste of his flesh from their earlier encounter. Cue massive cheers from the watching audience and a feeling of warmth towards the crocodile that has been waiting patiently for this opportunity.

Now for a happy ending with a twist! Having rescued Wendy and expecting her to resume her position as mother-figure to the 'Lost Boys', the ungrateful girl decides that her real place of home is back in Bloomsbury with her mother. Well would you credit it chaps but at the first sign of trouble she wants to go back to her mother. How often have we heard this before? Peter reluctantly takes her back and Mrs

Darling agrees to adopt the 'Lost Boys'. Peter refuses because he fears he will be caught and made into a man! The boy does not want to grow up. But he promises to return to Bloomsbury every spring to visit Wendy.

There is no traditional role for a Dame in the Peter Pan story so a character has been introduced in Pantomime. The most notable one is Laughing Water, a jolly and battered Indian squaw related to Tiger Lily. She often cracks jokes at her own expense and harbours a secret love for Smee, the timid pirate and second in command to Captain Hook. The interplay between them usually doubles as the comic duo. There is a substantial animal part in the role of Nana the dog who is the nursemaid and protector of the children. Nana reacts to dialogue and uses mime to show understanding and convey messages. She is treated as a human being by the Darling family.

The Peter Pan story is a great show because it has opportunities for adventure, sword fights, romance, songs and dance and is guaranteed to enchant children of all ages. Who cares if it is not strictly a Pantomime?

Puss in Boots: What is it about cats and Pantomime? First there was Tommy in 'Dick Whittington' and now we have got 'Puss in Boots'. This Pantomime is an adaptation of a traditional European fairy tale about a savvy feline who uses trickery and deceit to gain power, wealth and the marriage of his penniless and lowly born master to a beautiful Princess.

The story begins with the demise of an elderly widower who has three sons. He bequeaths each of them part of his estate. To the eldest boy he leaves the mill which is greeted magnanimously by the sons. To the middle boy he bequeaths his mules which could be useful to him in terms of earning an income. Finally to the younger son he leaves a cat! Now the boy is not entirely happy with this and considers killing the cat! But to his surprise the cat speaks to him and outlines a plan. If the boy will provide him with a pair of splendid boots and a sack, he might find that he might be of use to his new master. Thinking he has nothing to lose, the boy agrees to his demands and grants the cat his wishes.

Now what can a clever and crafty cat do with a pair of boots and a sack? Well go to work catching rabbits of course. Our wily feline friend catches a choice rabbit and heads off to the King's Palace and presents the Royal household with the cottontail. This is a wise investment as the King grants the cat an audience and asks who his master is? The cat replies the Marquis of Carabas, a fictitious title for his poor and penniless owner. Over subsequent days and weeks the cat manages to catch a whole host of game, using his sack, to keep the Royal household happy with a plentiful supply of fresh meat!

One day the King decides to take a ride in his carriage in the company of his beautiful daughter. The cat persuades his master to remove his clothes and enter a local river. The cat disposes of his master's clothes under a rock. The King's carriage passes by the river and the cat begins to scream for help and act in great distress. When the King stops to investigate, the cat tells him that his master has been bathing in the river and has been robbed of his clothing. The King has the young man brought from the river and dresses him in a splendid suit. Invited to ride in the carriage, the young man and the beautiful Princess fall in love.

But the cat has not finished yet. He hurries ahead of the carriage and orders the country folk along the road to tell the King that the countryside belongs to the Marquis of Carabas. Eventually the cat reaches a castle owned by an ogre. This ogre has the capability to transform himself into any creature known to man or cat. He shows this to the cat by turning into a lion which frightens our Puss. But undeterred by the sight of the lion, the cat tricks the ogre into turning himself into a mouse. Eager to impress the ogre does so and the cat proceeds to eat the mouse.

The King arrives at the castle that formerly belonged to the ogre and is told that the castle is the property of the Marquis of Carabas. Suitably impressed by the young man's providence the King offers the bogus Marquis the hand of his daughter in marriage. They are married and the cat lives a life of luxury in the Royal household where he runs after mice for his own pleasure!

Here is another Pantomime where there is no traditional Dame in the story so one has to be created. Generally the Queen can take the part and is portrayed as a bossy and fussy woman who rules the roost over the King and her subjects. She has a lot of comic interplay with the King who is hen-pecked and dominated by his wife. There may be an additional comic duo to supplement the King and Queens antics. Of course the part of Puss in Boots is wonderfully extravert and cheeky and seeks opportunities to put himself and his master in a good light with those of influence.

Mother Goose: Who was the real Mother Goose and did such a person really exit? These are two questions which have vexed Pantomime historians for decades. Mother Goose is suggested by some to be the real life author of several well-known nursery rhymes and fairy tales. But she is considered by others to be a fictional character who is symbolic of an 'everywoman' type of person; a good and humble person who is kind and considerate and is well-liked and good with children.

If a real Mother Goose did exist then some people believe the character is based on Elizabeth Goose, who lived in Boston during the 17th century. In 1692 she married Issac Goose, at the age of 27, adding her 6 children to his 10 to make a gigantic reconfigured family! However it has since been established that many of the fairy tales and nursery rhymes attributed to her were written before her birth. Elizabeth Goose was probably a good story teller and all round 'good egg' (no pun intended) and the guardian of a number of children who she entertained with exciting stories.

The 'Mother Goose' Pantomime, in several adaptations, first appeared over 100 years ago. However an earlier Pantomime called 'Harlequin and Mother Goose or the Golden Egg' was performed as early as 1806. The contemporary versions have Mother Goose living in Nurseryland and sharing the neighbourhood with several nursery rhyme characters. She is a poor yet popular woman who is good hearted and will do anything for anyone. However she is not endowed with good looks and her appearance is rather dowdy and shabby.

The penniless woman is being threatened with eviction after failing to meet her rental payments to the local squire. The bailiffs have visited and there seems no option for the good woman but to try to find alternative accommodation. It seems that her life has been scrambled (no pun intended) and her debts have boiled over! The Good Fairy observes Mother Goose's dilemma and knowing what a kind woman she is sends her hope in the form of Priscilla, a goose. Mother Goose adores Priscilla and accepts the goose as a true friend.

Later she discovers that the goose has the ability to lay golden eggs! All her money problems seem behind her now as she becomes financially more comfortable and is able to help her friends in the village who are also struggling during a period of increased rent demands and austerity. As you will know by now happiness is short-lived in Panto-land and dark forces are lurking in the background.

Enter the Demon King, a Villain who would not be out of place in a Bond movie. He discovers the source of Mother Goose's wealth and plots to gain possession of Priscilla for himself. A clever plan evolves in which he bets the Good Fairy that there is no one on earth who is happy with what they have, everyone wants more he argues and no one is content. The Fairy disagrees and cites Mother Goose as a prime example of someone who is happy with their lot! The cunning Demon King tempts Mother Goose with the one thing she does not have, youth and beauty. He persuades her to give him Priscilla in exchange for a visit to the fountain of youth.

Mother Goose gives him Priscilla and enters the fountain of Youth. She emerges as a beautiful young woman. However all her friends do not like her now. They want the old Mother Goose back and they want Priscilla as well. Realising that her vanity has got the better of her common sense Mother Goose must hatch a plan (no pun intended) to get the bird back. Depending on which version of the Pantomime you are watching, the process for the return of the goose varies. There may be a fight with the Demon King, a hearing at a court of Arbitration or a plea to the Good Fairy. Whatever the process is, the outcome is the same!

Priscilla and Mother Goose are re-united, the Demon King receives his come-uppence and Mother Goose goes back to being her good, old self. The message is that looks and beauty are not everything in life and there are more important things like friendship and family.

The role of Mother Goose is unique as it is the only Pantomime where the Dame is the main character. She always tries her best and looks on the bright side of life. The comic duo are usually a pair of bailiffs or 'broker's men' who try to extract the rent from the poor widow. Priscilla the Goose is a demanding role which requires the person inside the costume to dance as well as react to the dialogue of the other cast members.

Mother Goose is not as popular a Pantomime as it once was. It can be a very elaborate and extravagant show to perform, but it can be a delightful for children to see the cast of nursery rhyme characters in full costume and Priscilla is a big bird to enjoy!

Sleeping Beauty: Here is another classic fairy tale adapted into a Pantomime format which has proved very popular over the years. It enchants with the story of the love between a beautiful Princess and a handsome and brave Prince as well as the traditional elements of the Villain and the fight of 'Good' against 'Evil'. A King and Queen who are getting on in years eventually have a child they have always longed for. This is a time for celebration and joy throughout the kingdom.

They decide to have a spectacular party and christening and invite the great and the good from far afield to celebrate their good fortune. In the tradition of christenings held in this part of the world they invite the Good Fairies to attend and to endow the child with gifts. Unfortunately they forget to invite an Evil Fairy who feels slighted and offended by this shunning. As you know these kinds of ceremonies can be particularly sensitive to some people. However it seems they have chosen the wrong person to shun and the Evil Fairy casts a spell on the young Princess. Should the Princess prick her finger on the spindle of a spinning wheel she will die. The Good Fairy takes pity of the Royal couple and thinking that the spell is too harsh, modifies the curse so that the Princess will not die but will sleep for a 100 years when she will be awakened by the kiss from a handsome Prince.

The King issues a proclamation banning all spinning from the kingdom in an attempt to avert the spell being enacted. The Princess grows up into a beautiful and charming young lady and the kingdom goes through a period of happiness and joy. One day when the Royal couple are away doing royal duties, the Princess wanders around the Castle looking for things to do. She goes into a room she has not visited before and in one of them she comes across an old lady sitting at a spinning wheel. Intrigued by the actions of the spinning, the Princess asks the old lady if she might have a go. During the course of the spinning she unfortunately pricks he finger on the spindle.

The spell is enacted and the Princess falls asleep. Of course it is revealed that the old lady was merely a disguise for the Evil Fairy who wanted to trick the Princess. When the King and Queen return they are mortified by their daughter's condition and take her away to a chamber in the castle where she will be able to sleep for 100 years. They plea for help to the Good Fairy who is unable to break the spell but agrees to put everyone in the Castle to sleep for a 100 years so the Princess will not wake up alone and in distress.

As an extra layer of protection, the Good Fairy creates a deep forest around the castle with tall trees, brambles and thorns. So the inhabitants of the castle fall into a deep sleep and the forest grows to obscure any trace of what lies within it. Everything lies undisturbed until one day a Prince from a neighbouring kingdom gets lost in the forest whilst out hunting. He has heard tales of a sleeping beauty and is stunned when he discovers the walls of the protected castle. Using his sword he cuts through the brambles and the thorns until he finds the entrance to the castle. Then he wanders through the corridors passing the slumbering folk along the way.

Eventually he comes across the chamber of the sleeping Princess and astonished by her beauty steals a kiss! Immediately she wakes from her slumber and they fall in love. By now the rest of the castle's inhabitants have risen and the King and Queen are delighted that their daughter has been saved. The Prince and the Princess then marry to the sounds of great celebrations. The story may proceed with a sub-plot here where the Prince and Princess go off to seek revenge on the Evil Fairy and to banish her from their kingdom. Whatever the process, the outcome is that the couple will live happily ever after.

There is so much to like about Sleeping Beauty as a Pantomime. For example, the magical antics of the Good Fairy and the evil and jealous motivations of the Villainess. It has excitement galore with the cutting of the path through the forest to the castle entrance and the final showdown between the Prince and the Evil Fairy. Yet at the heart of the story is the beautiful Princess dressed in stunning gowns and the goodness she emits. Children love it and you should not be surprised to see them sitting wide – eyed in amazement as the story unfolds.

In early versions of the Pantomime the wicked Queen played the role of the Dame. More recently there has been the introduction of a Nanny or Nursemaid to the Princess. She is an accident prone meddler with a heart of gold. If there is not a definitive comic duo, the King and Queen have a good deal of comic interplay.

Jack and the Beanstalk: Generally considered to be a

tale of a simple lad made good, the story of Jack is actually based on a complex fairy story. Legend has it that in the past the country of Wales was terrorised by giants who rampaged the countryside and stole food and goods of value from the good Welsh folk. In the ancient story Jack is a Cornishman living near to Land's End and credited as the man who rid Wales of giants.

The first play based on the fairy tale was produced in 1773 and the first Pantomime production was staged in 1819. As part of Pantomime history it allegedly featured the first Principal Boy. There are several Pantomime adaptations but they generally follow a similar format. Jack is a young boy living with his widowed mother. Their only source of income is a dairy cow that produces the milk that Jack's mother sells. When the cow stops producing milk, Jack's mother tells him to take it to market to sell. On the way to the market Jack meets an old man who offers Jack some 'magic beans' in exchange for the heifer.

Not being the brightest button on the shirt, Jack agrees the exchange and returns home to his mother. The old lady is naturally very angry that Jack has swapped her precious cow for a handful of useless beans. She sends Jack to bed and throws the beans out the window! However when they wake up in the morning, a gigantic beanstalk has grown and stretches way up into the sky. Now Jack may not be such a clever lad but he is brave and adventurous. He climbs the beanstalk and discovers an enormous castle. Whilst wandering around the corridors of the castle Jack comes across a woman who is cooking in the kitchen.

Jack asks her for something to eat and the woman informs him that the castle belongs to a giant who is out hunting at the moment. She warns Jack that he should be gone before the giant returns. It turns out that she is the giant's wife. In some adaptations the giant has the name Blunderbone. Jack starts to eat and satisfy his hunger but after a while he hears the giant making a return to the castle. The giant's wife hides him in a cupboard. This giant has an acute sense of smell and immediately exclaims 'fee-fie-foe-fum, I smell the blood of an Englishman. Be he alive or be he dead, I'll grind his bones to make my bread!'

His wife assures him that there is no human being in the castle. Satisfied that his wife is not telling him porkies, the giant has his meal and goes to sleep. While the giant snoozes, Jack comes out of hiding. He notices several bags of gold by the giant and takes one. He descends down the beanstalk and presents the bag of gold to his mother, who as you can imagine is delighted!

The next day Jack climbs the beanstalk again and meets up with the giant's wife. Once more the giant is out on his rampages and Jack enjoys another meal in the kitchen before the giant returns. The giant is suspicious of a human presence but his wife reassures him that there is no one else in the castle. Jack hides in the cupboard again and while he is in there he sees the giant talking to a goose. The giant commands the goose to lay an egg. Jack notices that the egg the goose produces is actually a golden egg! The giant has his meal and falls asleep again. While he is asleep Jack comes out of hiding and steals the goose and once again descends the beanstalk and presents his mother with his latest prize.

The following day Jack ascends the beanstalk and once again enjoys a meal prepared by the giant's wife. When the giant returns he is again suspicious of the presence of an Englishman in his castle. Once again his wife reassures him and he settles down for his meal while Jack hides in the cupboard. Before the giant goes to sleep he picks up a harp and without playing any strings, the harp plays some beautiful music. This sends the giant into a deep sleep.

Jack comes out of the cupboard and takes the harp. He starts off towards the beanstalk but the sound of the harp as he runs along wakes the giant from his slumbers. The giant chases Jack and starts to climb down the beanstalk. But Jack is too quick for him and his descent is much faster. He calls for his mother to bring an axe and as the giant continues his descent, he chops at the beanstalk. This causes the giant to lose his grip and fall to his death.

With the beanstalk intact Jack is able to ascend the beanstalk one more time and rescue the giant's wife from her life in servitude. Enriched by the gold coins, the goose who lays the golden eggs and the harp that plays beautiful music, Jack and his mother are able to live happily ever after. I bet the mother on reflection is glad that Jack swapped the cow for the magic beans in the first place!

Jack's mother, Mrs Trott, usually plays the part of the Dame. A 'trot', in past times, was a nickname for an old 'hag'. She doubles up with her youngest son Simon as the comic duo. Of course there is a major animal part of the cow, which needs two people, and the heifer goes by the name of Daisy or similar. Interestingly there is no real principle girl so there may be reference to a local squire, who happens to have a beautiful daughter and Jack is in love with her. An alternative is a servant girl who is enslaved in the giant's castle. She aids Jack to hide and escape from the giant and Jack rescues her to live happily ever after.

Snow White and the Seven Dwarfs: This is a Pantomime with an interesting history. The story of 'Snow White and the Seven Dwarfs' originated from a series of fairy tales written and collected by the Brothers Grimm. It was first published by them in 1823 and was a well-established story across most of Europe after this time. The Pantomime is relatively new however and emerged after the success of the Walt Disney film in 1937. The film was a box office phenomenon and brought the story to a much wider audience.

The number of Dwarfs holds a magical significance as the number seven is regarded as a magical number in a number of different belief systems. For example most ancient astronomers believed there were seven planets, the great Jewish festivals last seven days and the 'seventh son of a seventh son' is thought to hold special powers according the Arabian legend. Whatever the significance the number seven sounds right in the title!

The story begins with the birth of a child to a Queen and King. They have been trying for a family for a long time and the child is seen as a precious gift to be treasured. The child's skin is so pale that they nickname her 'Snow White'. Sadly after the birth, the Queen is taken ill and dies. The King remarries but the new Queen, Snow White's step-mother is not a nice person. She is beautiful but vain and is jealous of the step-daughters close relationship to her father. She orders everyone to treat Snow White like a servant and gives her household chores to complete.

Snow White is a good girl and applies herself to her chores with diligence and fortitude. She thinks well about everybody and brings joy to the other people in the Palace who have to live with the Queen's bad temper. Soon Snow White grows into a beautiful young lady and is popular with everyone except the jealous Queen. Now the Queen is in possession of a magic mirror which can speak to her and give her advice. Each morning the Queen asks the mirror to confirm her vanity. She stands in front of the mirror and asks 'mirror, mirror on the wall, who is the fairest of them all?' Usually the mirror replies 'you are the fairest of them all.'

But one day the mirror replies 'Snow White is the fairest in the land'. The Queen is incensed and in her rage orders her huntsman to take to take Snow White into the forest and murder her. But the huntsman has a heart and he likes the girl, so he tells the girl the Queen's plans and orders her to run and hide. The Princess runs further into the forest and finds a small house. When she enters the house, she finds that it is very untidy.

Now being adept at domestic skills the young girl starts to clean up. She discovers that there is seven of everything including seven cups, seven plates and seven beds! When she has finished making the last bed she is so tired that she falls into a deep sleep. Snow White is awakened from her slumbers by seven Dwarfs who have returned to their house from a hard day's work. Some of the Dwarfs are unhappy with the intrusion into their home by this girl. But once Snow White tells them about the wicked Queen, the huntsman and her escape, they all agree that she should stay with them. In exchange for her board and lodgings Snow White agrees to cook and clean for them and the look after their home.

For a while an idyllic life of domestic bliss ensues. The Dwarfs grow to love Snow White and they are delighted with the cleanliness of the house and the delicious food she serves. The girl grows fond of her companions and is delighted with the love and affection she experiences from them. Although she misses her father and the other members of the Palace household, she does not miss the Queen.

But you cannot end a Pantomime with a story of domestic bliss! The Queen finds out that the Princess is still alive and distrustful of any of her servants to do her bidding; she decides that she will have to kill Snow White herself. She disguises herself as an old woman and poisons an apple which she places in her basket. She finds the Dwarf's house and knowing that they are out at work; she approaches the house and makes the acquaintance of Snow white who is busy with her housework.

They chat idly and the old woman offers Snow White the poisoned apple. As soon as the girl takes a bite from the fruit, she falls into a deep state of unconsciousness. The Dwarfs return from their hard day and work and discover the comatosed Princess. They immediately think she is dead and place her into a glass coffin which they position in a secluded part of the forest.

There she lies for several days until a young Prince, out hunting, finds the sleeping girl. Enchanted by her beauty he leans over and kisses her. This wakes the girl up and the young couple fall in love. Snow White tells the Prince her story and he decides that she should go and live in his kingdom where she will be safe from her evil step-mother. They marry and live happily ever after.

'Snow White the Pantomime' is unusual in its casting of traditional characters. There has often been no Dame in the story and when there is the role is one of a nurse to the Princess in the Palace. The comic turn is generally named 'Muddles' and he is usually Snow White's best friend at the Palace. These two characters appear in the first act of the Pantomime but have restricted roles when Snow White disappears into the forest and they cannot know the whereabouts of the Princess when she is living with the seven Dwarfs. Traditionally there is no major 'skin' part in the show but a troupe of children can be drafted into the Pantomime to play the animals of the forest.

Beauty and the Beast: The Pantomime is an adaptation of a traditional fairy tale written by the French novelist Gabrielle-Suzanne Barbot de Villeneuve and first published in 1740. This version was abridged and re-written in 1756 to produce the story most commonly retold.

A wealthy widowed merchant lives in a mansion with his children. The youngest daughter, Beauty is the most beautiful of his children as well as the most cultured and pure of heart. Her sisters are vain, selfish and treat beauty with distain. They all live a life of luxury until the merchant loses all his money when his ships are destroyed in a storm at sea. The family are forced to move to a smaller property and abandon their lavish life-style and adopt more austere conditions.

After a while the merchant discovers that one of his trade ships has survived the storm and the goods contained within it might be the key to free him and his family of their pauper lives. He sets off to the port and before he goes he asks his children what gifts they might like when he returns. The sisters request clothes and jewellery whilst Beauty asks for a single rose as the garden as the countryside around their current house cannot grow roses.

Sadly when the merchant reaches the port he discovers that the ship and his goods have been seized by his creditors to pay some of the debts he owes. Down-hearted and despairing the merchant heads for home. But in his confusion he loses his way in the forest. A storm breaks and he is grateful to see a castle ahead of him. When he arrives at the castle he finds the door open and a fantastic meal spread out on the table.

The merchant calls out but cannot find the owner of the castle. He enjoys the food and as he wanders the rest of the castle he finds a bed made up and waiting for him. He enjoys a good nights rest but is aware of the presence of another being in the castle. In the morning the merchant enjoys a good breakfast and on the way out of the castle spots a rose garden. He picks a rose remembering beauty's request. As soon as he plucks the rose for the bush a fierce Beast appears and threatens to kill him for abusing his hospitality by stealing a rose.

Pleading for his life the merchant begs the Beast to spare him and tells him the story of how his daughter requested a rose as a gift from him. The Beast relents and allows the merchant to go home but only on condition his daughter, Beauty, returns to the castle to stay with the Beast. The merchant agrees and returns home to his family. When he breaks the news that the Beast has spared his life, Beauty accepts the condition and goes to live with the Beast at his castle.

The Beast treats her well lavishing clothes and jewellery on her and meeting her wishes. She grows fond of the Beast but despite his advances, refuses a more romantic involvement. After a short time Beauty feels homesick and asks the Beast if she can return home to visit her father and her sisters. The Beast agrees as long as she returns within a week. He gives her two gifts to take with her; an enchanted mirror which allows her to see what is going on in the castle and a magic ring which allows her to return to the castle immediately.

Her father is delighted to see her but her sisters are jealous of her rich living style. They persuade Beauty to overstay her visit so that the Beast will become angry with her. But Beauty feels guilty and looks in the mirror to see what is happening at the castle. She is dismayed to see the Beast ailing with a broken heart and uses the ring to get back to the castle. When she sees the Beast she cries over his frail body for she realises she has fallen in love with the Beast. The tears fall onto the body of the Beast and as if by miracle, the Beast wakes up and is transformed into a handsome Prince.

The Prince explains to her that he was the subject of a wicked curse in which an Evil Fairy turned him into an ugly Beast because he refused to comply with her wishes. The curse could only be broken by finding true love despite his looks. The Prince and Beauty married and lived happily ever after.

The role of the Dame is usually someone who works for the merchant in his shop during the good times but goes with the family when they hit hard times. Her part may be supplemented by another worker who forms a comic duo with her. They can make fun of Beauty's sisters in a cheeky or insulting way.

Chapter Three
The Principal Boy

One of the intriguing aspects of the Pantomime is the reliance on a stock of main characters. Generally these characters are; the Principal Boy, the Dame, the Villain and the Good Fairy. This chapter will examine the origins and significance of each of these roles and identify some of the celebrated actors and actresses involved in the emergence of the parts.

One of the curious things to witness on stage is the part of the hero has traditionally been played by a female and is called the Principal Boy role. The ritual of women dressing up as men on stage started in the 18th century. Male roles played by women were known as 'breeches parts'. Cross dressing in theatre usually had been men dressing up as women and this practice continued into Pantomime. With the Principal Boy role, the romantic hero of every Pantomime story starts to be played by an attractive young lady dressed in a short tunic. The routine was at its most popular in the late Victorian era but still survives today.

The Victorian audience was not accustomed to viewing

the legs of a female. This was a period when the legs of furniture tended to be covered to avoid immodesty! It was an age of respectability and repressed sexuality. The Victorians were modest in their dress sense and a woman's legs were expected to be covered.

In contrast to the societal expectations however, the actress playing the 'breeches role' was encouraged to display as much leg as possible and was one of the factors which increased the popularity of Pantomime. The role requires the actress to retain their femininity but attention could be drawn to the legs by the character giving them a healthy slap of the thigh on each entrance to the stage. There is no attempt to disguise the fact that the male hero is a girl as the costumes would be feminised in their design.

The first Principal Boy took to the stage in 1819, when Eliza Povey played 'Jack' at the Drury Lane Theatre. There is little known about this young lady and her subsequent theatrical career but she was the forerunner to a whole succession of famous stars who donned the breeches (and later tunic) to play the hero in a number of different productions. There are many to choose from but only ten have been selected to give a flavour of the depth and range of talent needed to secure these roles.

One of the most famous Principal Boys in the Victorian era was **Nellie Farren** (1848-1906). She was born into a theatrical family and made her adult stage debut in 1864 following a career as a child star. Farren gained a large, mainly male audience, through her burlesque appearances at the Gaiety Theatre in London. Audience members would wear coloured scarfs to show support for their favourite actresses. Farren's colours were dark blue, light blue and white and she could look out over the audience and compare the popularity of her colours to those of other actresses.

Farren continued to work at the Gaiety for 25 years playing in comedies of all kinds as well as Shakespearean dramas. She suffered an attack of rheumatic fever in 1891 and her health forced her to retire from the stage in 1892. Her popularity was such that a gala benefit for her at the Theatre Royal, Drury Lane in 1898 raised the astonishing figure of £7,000 (equivalent to about £700,000 in 2015). Most of the notable actors of the time performed on her behalf.

Queenie Leighton (1874-1943) was born in London as Lilian Caroline Augusta Rickard. Her mother was an actress and Leighton became known as a child star making several appearances at the Drury Lane Theatre. She was known for the elegance of her performances and became a much loved Principle Boy in a number of Pantomimes including Prince Charming, Dick Whittington, Sinbad and Aladdin. However on a tour of Sinbad she had a stage accident and drew back on the demanding schedule of performances she had set herself.

Her first husband died fairly quickly into the marriage but in her later life she met Frederick Cockerill, a stage manager and she became heavily involved in the recruitment of young soldiers for the First World War whilst her husband served in the military.

Lil Hawthorne (1877-1926) was an American born

British stage music hall performer and Principal Boy who was involved in bringing the murderer Dr Crippen to justice. She started her variety career in America at the age of 14 as part of a song and dance trio 'The Hawthorne Sisters' with her sisters, Lola and Nellie. The trio transferred to London but following her sister's retirement Lil stayed on in London and made the first of her Principal Boy appearances in 1896. From then on she became a regular Pantomime actress.

Lil was a close friend of Cora Turner, the estranged wife of Dr Crippen. Concerned about her friends' disappearance, Lil and her husband pressed the police to investigate the matter more seriously than they were doing. They were able to prove, despite Crippen's asserting to the contrary, that his wife had not died in America. Lil Hawthorne died at the relatively young age of 49 in 1926.

Evelyn Laye (1900-1996) was a regular performer as Principal Boy. She had a background in musical theatre and light opera and had already performed as a star in a number of high profile shows in London and Broadway before traipsing the boards in Pantomime. Laye came from a theatrical family and was a child star making her stage debut at the age of 15. She was said to have a naturally projected singing voice and was passionate about her profession. Evelyn invested heavily in honing the skills of her craft by spending large parts of her salary on dancing, singing and combat lessons. Despite her success in musical theatre and films, she launched herself into Pantomime and became one of the most sought after Principal boys of her time.

Her career as a Principal boy coincided with the emergence of another famous actress and singer. **Adele Dixon** (1908-1992) was already a British musical theatre and film actress who had the honour of being the first performer on a British television broadcast. She sang the song 'Television' on the opening night of the historic BBC television broadcast in London on November 1936. Another prodigious child star, like Evelyn Laye, she made her first professional stage appearance at the age of 13. Adele was equally as well known in films and dramatic roles on stage. Later in her career she made her debut as a Principal Boy at the Sheffield Empire in December 1940 and went on to make a dozen appearances in the 'breeches role' including playing Prince Charming to Jack Buchannan's Buttons in a production of 'Cinderella'.

The actress **Noele Gordon** (1919-85) was famous for her portrayal of motel owner, Meg Mortimer (nee Richardson), in the long running television soap opera, Crossroads. But she had a distinguished career in musical theatre and television before this. Noele attended the Royal Academy of Dramatic Art and was a trained dancer as well. Prior to starring in Pantomime she had starred in nearly 1,000 performances of 'Brigadoon'.

She made her first appearance as a Principal Boy in 1943 at the Alexandra Theatre in Birmingham and she most notably appeared in the production of 'Humpty Dumpty' at the London Palladium in 1951. But her attention turned towards the rapidly evolving world of television. Noele went to New York to study television production and returned to the UK to help produce programmes on the newly created ATV Midlands. This was a commercial station which was keen to offer opportunities to push the boundaries of television presentation.

Noele left the production side of television work to host the first ITV chat show 'Tea with Noele'. During her time presenting the programme she became the first woman on ITV to interview a standing Prime Minister, Harold MacMillan. But it was the return to acting in 'Crossroads', which cemented her name in the public's eye.

When has a Dame got a background in being a Principal Boy? When it is **Dame Barbara Windsor** of course! Born in Shoreditch, she trained at the Alda Foster School in Golders Green and made her stage debut at 13 with her West End debut in 1952. She took the stage name 'Windsor' in 1953, inspired by the coronation of Queen Elizabeth.

Barbara played the role of Principal Girl in the production of 'Red Riding Hood' at the Shakespeare Theatre in Liverpool in 1955. But she became associated with the 'breeches' role in subsequent productions such as 'Aladdin', 'Cinderella' and 'Dick Whittington'. One of the great British stars she has been especially famous for the 'Carry On' films and for her long running portrayal as Peggie Mitchell in the BBC soap 'EastEnders'.

Born into an aristocratic Polish family, **Rula Lenska** went on to become one of Britain's most recognised actresses and one of the most enduring of Principal Boys in Pantomime productions. She was actually named Rose Maria Lubiensha at birth but this might have been difficult for theatre companies to reproduce on their posters! However she did renounce her Polish title as a Countess in the 1970s.

As an actress she has enjoyed considerable success on television and on stage in dramatic roles. Yet she has also played the Principal Boy role in most major Pantomime productions. Along the way she has had to share the stage with celebrities such as Mr Blobby, Neil and Christina Hamilton and various combatants for the television show 'Gladiators'. But she has shown an enthusiasm and resilience to be included in the list of Principal Boy greats.

Lorraine Chase moved from being a successful model into the acting world. She became well known for her strong cockney accent and use of cockney slang through a series of television adverts for Campari before embarking on her acting career. Her stage work has included 'Pygmalion', 'Little Shop of Horrors' and 'Me and My Girl'. But she has been a consistent performer in Pantomime making the transition from Principal Boy to more adult parts such as the Villainess. Lorraine has appeared in several television series, most notably in the role of Steph Forsythe in 'Emmerdale' from 2002-2006. She is a patron of the theatre charity 'The Music Hall Guild of Great Britain and America'.

The talented dancer, singer and actress **Bonnie Langford** first came to prominence as a child star in the 1970s. She attended the Arts Educational School and the Italia Conti Academy and was brought to the public's attention when she won the television talent show 'Opportunity Knocks'. This led to parts in the television series 'Just William' and the film 'Bugsy Malone' as well as numerous musical theatre productions.

Between 1986 and 1987 she played the part of Mel, companion to the sixth and seventh Doctor in the science fiction series 'Dr Who'. She has subsequently appeared in several top-rated musical theatre shows such as 'Chicago' and 'Guys and Dolls', whilst continuing to have strong presence in television work and dramatic stage parts.

Her all round singing, dancing and acting talents have made her a natural Principal Boy. She has done Pantomime regularly and has been 'Peter Pan', 'Aladdin' and 'Dick Whittington' as well as a host of other roles.

Recently there has been a trend towards male Principal Boy with pop stars and soap stars playing the role. So the tradition of the 'breeches role' is gradually eroding and the prospect of seeing a glamourous female showing her shapely legs and slapping her thigh on entering the stage may be a thing of the past.

The Principal Girl role is more straight-forward in performance. She is played by a female and is often the title of the Pantomime such as 'Cinderella', 'Snow White' or 'Sleeping Beauty'. The character tends to be pure, honest and virtuous. Of course she worships the hero who frequently has to carry out feats of daring to rescue our poor heroine who has been captured or put under a spell by the evil Villain.

Chapter Four
The Dame

The tradition of men playing women in the theatre has a long history. Females did not really enter theatrical work in the UK until the 17th century. Up until then it was not considered acceptable for females to pursue a career on stage. When they did start to appear, the generally younger females did not want to play the parts of the old maid or the roles of witches. So these roles still tended to be played by men.

The character is usually old and matronly and may be obsessed by finding love. They come in several types; the working class, plain and hard-done by woman, the beautiful but haughty or the ugly and the grotesque. But the character remains consistent with a bawdy sense of humour, outrageous costumes, slapstick scenarios and strong interaction with the audience.

The role of the Dame is best played when it is clear that the gender playing the part is male. There is no attempt to disguise this and all aspects of the character's physical appearance tend to be exaggerated with big make-up and costumes. There is a high degree of melodrama with heightened emotions and sensational reactions to minor events.

During the 18th and 19th century the Dame became the vehicle for the great variety acts. The Dame may not be central to the storyline but she choreographs the other members of the cast and elicits loud and repetitive responses from the audience. During a performance there are usually a large number of costume changes. Each costume will be flamboyant and outrageous. The list of famous Dames is long, so it is necessary to select ten performers to display the skills they employed and elicit what they brought differently to the role.

It would be impossible to write about the emergence of the Pantomime Dame without referring to **Joseph Grimaldi** (1778-1837). He was the most popular English entertainer of the Regency era. Grimaldi was born into a show business family with a father who was apparently a tyrant. He began to perform as a child and made his stage debut at Drury Lane at the age of eight.

Grimaldi gained prominence as a clown in the tradition of the Harlequinade. His style of clowning has its origins in the Commedia dell'arte of the sixteenth century and the Harlequinades. He developed many of the classic components of the clown's performance and his name was shortened to 'Joey' which is still the name associated with the concept of the clown. Towards the end of the 1790s he starred in a Pantomime version of 'Robinson Crusoe' but it was in his first real triumph 'Mother Goose' that he laid the foundations for the modern Pantomime.

His clowning was physical and energetic and he developed the tradition of the audience singing along and participating in the action. In 1812 he donned the skirts of the Queen in 'Harlequin and the Red Dwarf' and was later to play the Baroness in 'Cinderella'. Here began the transition from clown to Pantomime Dame with the exaggerated sense of dress, crude and haughty characterisation, audience responses to catch-phrases and flamboyant and rapid costume changes. However the Dame did not fully emerge until the 1860s with the emergence of the variety music hall stars.

Herbert Campbell (1844-1904) starred for 40 years at the Theatre Royal, Drury Lane in Pantomimes predominately as a Dame. After a brief stint in office work Herbert set his sights on a theatrical life. He formed a very successful partnership with another Pantomime regular, Dan Leno, when they were cast together from 1888. Before that Campbell had been a successful comedian and singer on the Variety Hall circuits. He established himself after unsuccessful periods with others.

Campbell was a large and tall man who had a very strong singing voice. He encouraged the audience to accompany him and to sing the refrains of the chorus. By contrast Leno was small and diminutive and this made the partnership a visual feast of slapstick and humour. They specialised in ad-libbing, often deviating from the scripts at will and presenting a new performance each time. He gave his last performance in during the 1903-04 Pantomime season.

There are few classic Pantomimes that Campbell did not perform in. His repertoire included; 'Babes in the Wood', 'Cinderella', 'Humpty Dumpty', 'Aladdin' and 'Dick Whittington'. Outside of performing he was a big supporter of charities which helped performers who were infirm or elderly. In 1898, with the help of Leno and another star, Johnny Danvers, he built the Granville Theatre in Fulham. A commemorative plaque was placed outside his former home in Hackney as a mark of his importance to British theatre.

Campbell's long-time partner in Pantomime was **Dan Leno** (1860-1904). Although they shared the stage on numerous occasions, their comic styles and approaches were very different but strangely complimentary. The chemistry between them must have been an overwhelming theatrical experience. Leno was born George Wild Galvin but adopted his stage name early on in his career. His parents were from a theatrical background and he was encouraged to entertain as a child, making his first solo appearance on stage at the age of nine. As a teenager he developed a reputation for his clog dancing and formed a duo with his brother. It was not long before he was the star of his families act.

He became one of the most highly paid comedians of his generation and his music hall act evolved a unique style where he would talk about everyday life and often mundane subjects mixed with comic songs and surreal characterisations. He created a wide range of male and female characters to illustrate his stories.

He was an ideal candidate for Pantomime and made his

first appearance in Liverpool in 1865. The following year he appeared as Dame Durden in 'Jack and the Beanstalk' at London's Surrey Theatre. By 1888 Leno began the first of his hugely successful Pantomime partnerships with Herbert Campbell and Harry Nicholls. The partnership continued for the next fourteen years becoming one of the most enduring acts in theatre history.

Such was the measure of their success that Leno had to reduce his music hall appearances as a consequence. He was noted for giving each of his Dames' a personality of their own rather than give a stereotypical portrayal. His demise was slow and insidious and due mainly to his increasing use of alcohol. His erratic behaviour towards his fellow performers made him a difficult person to work with. But in sobriety he was remorseful and apologetic.

An unfulfilled obsession to be taken seriously as a dramatic actor and his deteriorating physical and mental health led to his admission to the Camberwell House Asylum in 1903. He returned to a triumphant Pantomime stage in 1904 when he secured his release from the Asylum but he died of ill-health the following year. His death was treated as national news with fitting tributes from fellow performers, theatre critics and newspapers. He was as big a loss to the world of Pantomime as his partner, Campbell, who died in the same year.

One of the great Pantomime Dames to emerge in the early part of the 20th century is **George Lacy** (1904-1989). George was born in London and made his stage debut at the age of 14. Lacy performed his first Dame role at the age of 24 and went on to appear in over 60 Pantomimes until his death in 1989.

Much of his Dame's comedy arrived from the fact that he delivered working class gags with a posh accent. He was also a strong believer in the importance of costume. He is credited with beginning the tradition of appearing in a new costume for each scene. His flamboyant use of material and colourful designs were a big hit with audiences and his snooker table costume was such a success that he wore it for eleven consecutive years as he toured the country.

Lacy had such a reputation that he was perceived by some to be the finest Dame of his generation. The role of 'Mother Goose' was one he made his own. He frequently wrote his own scenes and songs with adaption of the script to suit his characterisation. His final Pantomime was performed in 1984 at the King's Theatre, Southsea, where at the age of 80, he performed his last 'Mother Goose'.

The performer who brought the most glamour and grandeur to the role of the Pantomime Dame was undoubtedly **Danny La Rue** (1927-2009). Born in Cork, Ireland as Daniel Patrick Carroll, his family moved to England when Danny was six. He became interested in amateur dramatics and was often cast in the female role as there was a shortage of girls to play the parts.

In his later stage career, La Rue developed a unique routine as a female impersonator. He disliked the term 'drag-artist' and preferred to call himself as a 'comic in a frock'. Danny La Rue appeared in over 45 Pantomimes over a career of 60 years. He started as an ugly sister in 'Cinderella', forming a successful partnership with a more experienced actor called Alan Haynes.

But La Rue took the role of the Dame to another level with his glamourous and elegant portrayals. He brought sophistication and glittering spectacle to his shows and insisted on expensive and stylish costumes. By doing so he transformed the tradition of the Dame from one of the 'drag-act' persona, previously seen as coarse and vulgar, into something that achieved refinement and classiness. He played the female role straight making it clear he was a man and definitely not a woman using his gravelly voice to reinforce the masculinity of his alter-ego.

An all-round entertainer who performed successfully across a number of mediums was the Scotsman **Stanley Baxter**. Born in Glasgow in 1926, Baxter has stayed true to his Scottish roots but became nationally known across the UK through his television, stage and radio work. He was encouraged to take to the stage by his mother and like many entertainers of his generation; he honed his skills during his National Service duties working with other performers such as Kenneth Williams. By the end of his military career he was confident enough to work with the Citizen's Theatre in Glasgow before moving into radio with the BBC Scotland show 'It's All Yours'.

Baxter was a noted impersonator of characters including George Formby and Marlene Dietrich. Between the 1960's and the 1980's he enjoyed his most successful period when he starred in a number of spectacular comedy specials. Often he played over 40 different characters in his one hour specials and is credited for the use of the split-screen technique of filming allowing up to 4 characters to appear side by side on screen.

His Pantomime performances were legendary in Scotland. For many years he alternated his Pantomime appearances between Glasgow and Edinburgh. His Pantomimes were lavish and emulated the detail and expense of his television shows. One of his unique contributions was the use of 'Parliamo Glasgow' in which he demonstrated the art of speaking Glaswegian as a foreign language. These became a standard feature of his song sheets to which the audience were invited to sing along to!

Born in Collyhurst, Manchester, **Les Dawson** (1931-1993) was a relative late-comer to the world of entertainment. His first job was in the parcel department of the Manchester Co-op and his other jobs included being a journalist at the Bury Times. Encouraged by his mother, Les took up the piano and gained a good deal of competency. In fact he started out in show business as a pianist and evolved his comedic act by playing wrong notes and then complaining to the audience about his incompetence.

He made his television debut on the talent show 'Opportunity Knocks' in 1967. Television was his natural medium and he was soon hosting his own shows and the popular quiz show 'Blankety Blank'. His greatest influence was the northern comic Norman Evans whose stage shows included the creation of norther characters such as Joe Ramsbottom and Fanny Fairbottom. During his television shows he created a sketch in which he played the character of a northern woman, Ada, who would engage in comic dialogue with another northern character, Cissie, played by Roy Barrowclough.

His first Pantomime was in Doncaster and he extended the role of Ada into his performance as a Dame. His greatest success was as 'Nurse Ada' in 'Babes in the Wood' which beat all previous box-office records and ran for 10 weeks at the Manchester Palace Theatre. A speciality of Les Dawson was his quick witted puns and play on words as well as his facial gurning.

A favourite on television, **John Inman** (1935-2007), made his name on the BBC sit-com 'Are You Being Served? ' He became one of the finest Dames of his generation and formed a striking impression with his inventive and pristine costumes, many of which he designed himself. Inman formed a successful partnership with another sit-com star, Barry Howard, from 'Hi-De-Hi', when they teamed up as the ugly sisters in 'Cinderella'.

Born in Preston, his family moved to Blackpool when John was still young. He was determined to make his name as an actor and subsidised his stage career by taking a variety of jobs including window-dressing and shop work. Inman made his stage debut at the age of 13. In order to pursue his dream he went to London where parts were more available. He worked in several West End productions as well as regional repertoire.

When his partnership with Barry Howard folded, he went to appear in many of the traditional Pantomime productions. John Inman was acknowledged as a classic

Dame specialising for many years in the role of 'Mother Goose' and then 'Widow Twankey' in Aladdin. In all he appeared in over 40 Pantomimes and attracted a strong and loyal following. Sadly he died in 2007 at the age of 71.

Although not a national name, **Berwick Kaler**, has a unique place in the history of the Pantomime Dame. He writes, directs and stars in the annual Pantomime in York at the Theatre Royal. Here he has a strong, loyal and dedicated following. The Pantomimes he creates are based on the traditional form of the art and he avoids celebrity stars and risqué humour in his productions.

Born in Sunderland, Kaler moved to London to pursue his dream of being on stage. With no formal training he was offered work at 'Dreamland' in Margate as jack of all trades where he was expected to perform a variety of theatrical parts. This comprehensive entry into theatrical work served him well and gave him the confidence to carry on with his dream.

He arrived in York in 1976 to perform in a stage play but was also offered the part of the Dame in the annual Pantomime. He initially refused but a change of mind cemented his future in York. Dis-satisfied with the quality of the scripts he asked to perform. Kaler started to write his own scripts and adapt traditional stories to incorporate local or contemporary scenarios.

He has appeared in nearly 50 Pantomimes and the annual role in the Christmas Pantomime has resulted in him being awarded the Freedom of the City of York. As part of his traditional emphasis he throws Wagon Wheels to the audience and gives a bottle of beer of Newcastle Brown Ale to a father in the stalls. A truly unique contributor to the art of being a Pantomime Dame, he deservedly occupies a place in the renowned Dames of Pantomime.

It is fitting to end the list of great Dames with the person known as the 'Grand Dame of Pantomime', **Christopher Biggins**. Born in Oldham but brought up in Salisbury, the young Biggins showed an early interest in drama. His first lead role was at the age of 17. Since then he has enjoyed a successful career in television including appearances in the situation comedies 'Porridge' and 'Whatever Happened to the Likely Lads?, as well as dramatic roles in 'Poldark' and 'I, Claudius'.

He started in Pantomime in 1965 when he appeared in 'Dick Whittington'. Since then he has appeared in the annual show every year, bar one. Biggins has announced his intention to retire from the Pantomime stage in 2017. This will be nearly 40 years of playing all the classic roles such as 'Widow Twankey', 'Mother Goose' and 'Sarah the Cook'.

As a master of the art, Biggins suggests there are certain things that make the role successful. First, the costumes should be funny and outrageous and change with every entrance. Second the Dame should never forget they are a man in a frock, and not a drag act. Third the Dame must have a 'catch-phrase' and frequently use it to interact with the audience. He uses the 'catch-phrase' of 'Naughty, Naughty' in all his portrayals.

This quick guide through the history of those who have donned the Dame persona shows that although the role may appear the same, there is tremendous variation in how the various actors have interpreted it over the years. Each of them have brought something different to the role or developed the role in ways that are truly unique. The Dame is central to the success of any Pantomime as the action generally revolves around them as they orchestrate the audience in to suspending their belief and entering into the magical world unfolding before them on stage.

In contrast to the Principal Boy they emphasise their masculinity by their femininity, often being outrageously male in a female guise but searching for love from a male member of the cast who can offer them a life outside the one they are experiencing. Usually they are desperate for love but have an inflated sense of their own beauty and attractiveness. Despite their human frailties and vulnerabilities, the Dame should be the most lovable performer on stage.

Chapter Five
The Villain

Imagine walking onto a stage and being almost immediately disliked by everyone in the audience. As you walk on you are greeted by 'booing' and 'hissing' and no one is acting as if they would vote for you to stay in the Pantomime equivalent of the 'Big Brother' household. Such is the experience of being the Villain in a Pantomime. For the Villain must focus their attention in the undoing and demise of the hero of the piece. They must be dastardly and cunning, mischievous and sinister in their actions and thoughts. Primarily they are there to thwart the ambitions and the desires of the hero.

The exact guise and name of the Pantomime Villain may differ but the characteristics of the antagonist is always the same! They must be as evil as possible and more evil than anyone else in the world. The Villain is evil for its own sake and enjoys being an evil person. He or she (for the Villain can be male or female) mistreats his henchmen or subordinates and enjoys doing so. They laugh at the suffering of others and their misfortunes. However whilst the Villain has an elevated and superior opinion of themselves, they are often somewhat incompetent and will inevitably be outwitted or outfoxed by the hero of the Pantomime.

There is a marked contrast between the forces of 'Good' and 'Evil' that is in conflict in any Pantomime. 'Good' is represented by the characters of the 'Good Fairy' or the 'Fairy Godmother'. Their role is to help the hero to realise their ambitions and to ensure that love and romance can evolve. However they are battling against the evil of the Villain throughout the Pantomime and it is this battle, rather than the story of the hero, which is the central moral being acted out. 'Good' always triumphs over 'Evil'!

Whilst the location and topicality of the story may vary, certain stage directions nearly always hold strong. Good always enters from stage right and Evil from stage left. The tradition of 'Evil' entering from the left or sinister side dates back to the medieval mystery plays. The stage direction echoes the medieval belief where the entrances to heaven and hell were placed on these sides. Tradition always dictates that the Villain will always enter first, followed by their adversary, the 'Good Fairy'.

The story nearly always revolves around the tried and tested formula of 'Good' conquering 'Evil' and requires the Villain to make all the innocent character's lives a misery. Usually by the end of the show, all the baddies and their henchmen will either have been destroyed or made to see the errors of their ways and turned into reformed characters!

Unlike the Dame or the Principal Boy, the Pantomime Villain does not always get the applause and acclaim they are due. Often the role is played by a classically trained actor or actress rather than a television or reality show performer. As such their star does not always shine as brightly as the other lead parts but they are an essential component of the annual Christmas show and we will celebrate the unsung heroes and heroines of dastardly deeds here.

Over several decades the annual show at York Theatre Royal has built up a formidable reputation for delivering the best in traditional family fun. It has the advantage of a stable group of performers who return most years to contribute to the constancy which the audience demands. Among this group is the redoubtable **David Leonard**, who has been playing the part of the Villain for over 20 years.

He trained at the Guildford School of Acting and has established himself in a number of top West End shows including Miss Trunchbull in 'Matilda'. But he has also worked consistently since graduating in work on stage, television and musicals. But each year he returns to York, other work commitments allowing, to star along the celebrated Dame, Berwick Kaler.

Leonard has expressed a high degree of honesty about playing the role of the Villain. He suggests it is the repertory nature of the York Theatre set-up that is one of the attractions for him coupled with the familiarity of the audience expectations of a traditionally focused Pantomime. But the demands of the York Theatre Royal production, 75 performances every year, places a burden on an actors physical health and their voice and preparation is key to sustaining credible performances.

Unlike the Dame and Principal Boy, there is no gender division to play the Villain; it can be cast as either a male or a female. One of the most successful female portrayals was the late **Marti Caine** (1944-1995). Born Lynne Shepherd in Sheffield, the young Marti worked in a variety of jobs whilst trying to achieve her ambitions to become a talented singer and comedienne. These included croupier and petrol pump attendant. At the age of 18 she made her professional appearance as a comedienne and spent the next 15 years playing the notoriously difficult Northern Working Men's Club circuit.

Starting as more of a singer, she developed her own style of humour by combining an appealing dizziness with an endearing vulnerability. Glamourous young women in figure-hugging mini-dresses were a novelty at the time and Marti was able to walk the tight-rope between challenging the beer swilling males with their chauvinistic attitudes and affirming pre-conceptions of her feminine charms.

At the age of 30 she entered and won the television talent show 'New Faces'. From this she made numerous television appearances and was eventually rewarded with her own show, 'The Marti Caine Show' on BBC2. Being a singer, dancer and comedienne made her a natural for Pantomime and she starred in a number of productions. But it was her portrayal of the 'Red Queen' in 'Snow White and the Seven Dwarves' which cemented her Villainous role in Pantomime. A longer career in Pantomime beckoned but this was cut short by an earlier than expected death at the age of 50.

One of the strengths of the Christmas Pantomime season in the UK is the depth of regional repertory troupes which return year on year to perform at the less attractive venues and who build up a sustained and loyal following. These theatres are generally outside of London and the big cities but they cater for a local population. The advantages of this are that they are able to incorporate local stories into the plot and use the regional dialect to interact with the audience.

One of the more successful locations is the Oldham Coliseum where the resident Dame Fine Time Fontayne writes and performs the annual Pantomime. The resident Villain there is played by **Andonis Anthony** who has a strong background in theatre in the Northwest as well as a good television profile. He has appeared in 'Coronation Street' on a number of occasions in different roles, as well as 'Emmerdale' and 'The Bill'. But he has a formidable stage presence with appearances in 'A Taste of Honey' and 'The Accidental Death of an Anarchist'.

During his Pantomime career in Oldham he has played all the major Villains such as Captain Hook, King Rat and the Evil Demon of Discontent in 'Mother Goose'. The familiarity between performers and the audience usually means that the dialogue is more interactive than celebrity driven shows and the audience feel more a part of the plot. The foundations of the Pantomime can be built on each year by having a coherent and successful partnership between the main characters and this is what the regional theatres are able to achieve. A further strength is that the shows give regular seasonal employment to actors who may not be household names but have a strong theatrical reputation.

One of the hallmarks of a great Pantomime Villain is the versatility of talents that a performer must have to successfully embrace the role. One of the most versatile people to play the Villain in one of the most flourishing annual Pantomimes is **Kit Hesketh-Harvey**. Born in what is now known as Malawi into a Foreign Office family, Hesketh-Harvey was educated as a senior chorister at Canterbury Cathedral and later Tonbridge School in Kent. It was at Cambridge University where his theatrical ambitions took off as he joined the famous Cambridge Footlights Dramatic Club.

He has enjoyed a very successful career as a performer, writer and adapter of major theatrical works and his range spans television, theatre and radio as well as live performance. Perhaps he is best known as one half of the cabaret acts, Kit and the Widow and Kit and McConnel who are very much in demand at the Edinburgh Fringe Festival and live entertainment circuits.

Each year Hesketh-Harvey takes time out from his busy schedule to appear as the Villain at the Yvonne Arnard Theatre in Guildford. This is recognised as one of the most prestigious and celebrated Pantomimes in the UK. He always plays the Villain and brings to the role his own perspective. In a self-penned article he describes how he plays the role on two different levels. On the one hand he has to give a convincing and scary portrayal which tells the story as powerfully as possible to enthral the children and keep them pleasantly scared. On the other hand the Villain is delivering a wink to the adults in the audience to acknowledge the silliness and absurdity of it all.

It is the strength of the Guildford Pantomime that it can attract such an esteemed and influential performer as Hesketh-Harvey back each year. Certainly it is respected and celebrated in the theatre world by critics as one of the top Pantomimes to see each year. Like most of the regional shows the presence of a consistent and continuous set of performers is part of the attraction for audiences who come from a wide geographical area to see the show in Guildford each year.

Sometimes it is to an actor's advantage to be known for playing the Villain in other mediums when they come to play the baddie in Pantomime. Such is the case with **Todd Carty** who flourished in television as the devious policeman, Gabriel Kent, in the ITV drama 'The Bill'. Born in Limerick, in Ireland, he moved to England with his family and showed an aptitude for the stage at an early age. He learnt quickly and put into practice his drama teachers advice to 'turn up on time, learn your lines and don't bump into the furniture'.

Success came quickly when he was cast as the 'bad boy' in the role of Tucker Jenkins in the BBC Children's drama series 'Grange Hill' and the subsequent follow-up 'Tuckers Luck'. Carty graduated to the cast of 'EastEnders' playing the part of Mark Fowler, a complex character who occasionally crossed over to the dark side of life. He played the part of Mark Fowler for 13 years and then left to play the bent and sociopathic copper, Kent, for a further two years.

Obviously his appearances as the Villain in Pantomime were a natural progression. He made his debut as King Rat at the Wycombe Swan Theatre in 2005. Since then he has starred as other Villains such as Abanazaar in 'Aladdin' and Ferdinand Fleshcreep in 'Jack and the Beanstalk'. He combines his work in Pantomime with stage, television and radio appearances but has recently moved behind the camera to direct short films.

One of the challenges facing the Pantomime actor is the seasonal nature of the work. During the winter season they can be assured of theatre work but what do they do in the months in between. One of the most versatile artists to manage this conundrum is **Steve Arnott**. During the 'quiet' periods, when he is not frightening children as a Pantomime Villain, he turns his hand to constructing and designing sets for shows, stage managing productions, joinery and other construction skills and as well as all this he still finds the time to co-author Pantomime scripts under the banner of 'Grimaldi'.

Furthermore he has also covered every aspect of the theatre from performing, directing and stage management. This is a truly versatile theatrical wizard who steps onto the stage at the Newcastle Theatre Royal annual Pantomime. He actually started off his show business career as a voice-over artist before making the transition to stage. He initially performed as the Dame in Pantomimes and made the shift into becoming the despicable Villain. It is this portrayal which has endeared him to audiences in the North-East and he has become the regular scoundrel of the annual Tyneside season.

Steve receives rave reviews not just for his performances as the Villain but also for the make-up which he applies himself. In order to help create his character he takes great care of his costume and cosmetic application. His advice is the take the make-up off between each performance and to start afresh with a new application. A real example of a theatrical professional who uses all his talents to ensure his all year round employment and a treasure of the Pantomime scene.

Another of the many females to make her mark as a Pantomime Villain, **Anita Dobson** has worked steadily in theatre and television. Born in Stepney Anita attended the Webber Douglas Academy of Dramatic Arts in London and went on to gain experience in a wide range of stage and television roles with limited success. She eventually was rewarded for her hard work by landing the role of Angie Watts, the highly strung, alcoholic landlady of the Queen Vic in the BBC soap opera EastEnders. In one episode on Christmas Day 1986, she took part in the scenes where her screen husband, Dirt Den Watts, handed her their divorce papers. The episode recorded an audience viewing figure of 30.15 million viewers, a figure unsurpassed in television soap history.

But her talents extend much wider. She has made West End appearances in the National Theatre production of 'Frozen' as well as 'Chicago' and 'Hamlet'. In 2012 she made her Royal Shakespeare Company debut in the revival of 'The Merry Widows of Windsor'. Anita is also a talented singer and dancer.

She is proud of her Pantomime career and thinks it is a way of giving something back to a loyal audience and encouraging children to access the theatre as Pantomime may be their first introduction to this world. Her performances are known to be emotionally intense with strong emphasis on audience participation particularly encouraging the audience to 'boo' and 'hiss' to ever louder crescendos.

Known with affection around the world as 'The Hoff', **David Hasselhoff** has a distinctive role as the Pantomime Villain with his self-depreciating and self-critical humour. Here is an actor who can see the funny side of his fame yet remain committed to giving his audience value for money with his performances. Born in Baltimore, Maryland, in the United States of America, the 'Hoff' had early ambitions to perform in Pantomime with his first appearance in 'Peter Pan' at the age of seven.

He studied at Oakland University before graduating with a Degree in Theatre from the California Institute of the Arts. Tall and muscular, he was able to secure roles in television work relatively early on in his career. But he rose to prominence and international stardom playing Michael Knight in the fantasy series 'Knight Rider' and as LA County lifeguard Mitch Buchannan in the very popular series 'Baywatch'.

David was also well known for his stage work. He had a successful run playing the male lead in the musical

'Chicago' and the Las Vegas production of 'The Producers'. But never shy of putting himself forward he launched another successful side of himself, and his family, through reality television series such as 'The Hasselhoffs'. If that was not enough he also launched a very successful singing career particularly in Europe where he achieved triumphant sales of his albums.

Always feeling accepted in the UK there were inevitable offers to star in Pantomime and he made his debut playing 'Captain Hook' in 'Peter Pan' in 2010. Since then he has returned to play the role of the dastardly Captain every year at different venues across the country. He cuts a swagger in the role and makes several references to his own fame and his past successes on television. The audiences love him for the way he carries the part and he brings a very different approach to the Pantomime stage.

Used to hearing the 'boos' and 'hisses' of audiences through his association with 'Strictly Come Dancing', **Craig Revel Horwood**, is an ideal candidate to play the role of Villain in the Pantomime. Born in Ballarat, Australia, he started his career as a dance in Melbourne before moving to London to take advantage of the greater opportunities there. He has expanded his repertoire to include choreography and stage direction. Horwood has been involved in a number of West End and theatrical productions including; 'Spend, Spend, Spend', 'My One and Only', 'West Side Story' and 'Miss Saigon'.

But he is most familiar to UK audiences as one of the judges in 'Strictly Come Dancing' where he is regarded as the harshest of the judging panel with his strong adherence to the application of the rules of ballroom dancing. He seems to relish the audience reaction to his comments on the contestant's performance and placing himself in the role of Villain on the show.

He made his Pantomime debut in 2009 when he played the part of the Wicked Queen in 'Snow White and the Seven Dwarves' in Llandudno. He has reprised this role in subsequent Pantomimes around the UK. Lately he has moved on to play Captain Hook in 'Peter Pan'. Building on his 'Strictly' persona, Horwood is the Villain everyone loves to hate and has the audience eating out of the palm of his hand with the frequent use of his catch-phrase 'Fab-u-las'.

Imagine the main characteristics of a Pantomime Villain to be a big, booming voice, a large stage presence, a robust swagger and the ability to be both frightening and comical, then the job description perfectly fits the well-known British actor, **Brian Blessed**. Born in Mexborough in Yorkshire, he showed an acute talent for acting in school productions before receiving his training at the Bristol Old Vic. Blessed has been appearing regularly on our television, stage, cinema and radio mediums since his long running appearances as PC 'Fancy' Smith in the BBC television series Z-Cars from 1962 until 1965.

Anyone who has witnessed his portrayal of Prince Vulcan in the film 'Flash Gordon' will have recognised his ability to be both frightening and comical and to imprint memorable catch-phrases in an audience's heads with a minimum of effort. Blessed's credentials for Pantomime Villain are exceptional and like with any role he has portrayed in his long and distinguished career, he brings to the Christmas stage his unbounding energy and professionalism.

Wherever he appears, he roars on to the stage and draws upon his own love of Pantomime and the pivotal role it has played in his life. Blessed remembers going to see the annual Christmas shows in Sheffield as a youngster and the magic of the sights, sounds and sets he witnessed were instrumental in his decision to become an actor.

But it is not only his stage presence in roles such as Captain Hook in 'Peter Pan' which draw gasps and copious bouts of 'booing' and 'hissing' from the audience. His versatility is shown in his distinctive and notable voice-over work as the Giant Blunderbone in 'Jack and the Beanstalk' where he does not even have to be on stage to be frightening and entertaining! A true Giant of the Pantomime stage!

Chapter Six
The Good Fairy

The most important element of the Pantomime is the battle between 'Good' and 'Evil', with 'Good' emerging triumphant. The Good Fairy or Fairy Godmother embodies all that is righteous and has a special role in watching over the hero. Blessed with magical powers they can act as a mentor or parent to the hero and dress in glamourous and sparkly ways. She plays little part in the action, instead greeting the audience at the beginning of the performance and acting as a narrator between scenes, often speaking in verse.

The only exception to these defined roles in when she sometimes uses her magical powers to rescue the hero, just when it looks like all hope has been lost. This is known as the 'deus ex machina' device, in drama or fiction, where an act of magic, an event or the introduction of a new character is suddenly introduced to provide a contrived solution to an otherwise unsolvable problem. The device usually appears in a chaotic situation and restores calm and order.

Given the glamour required of such a part, the role has

tended to be played by actresses and reality stars who may have limited acting experience or training. The actress must give the aura of being good and pure but worldly wise and opposed to the forces of evil gaining ascendancy in the story. There are several famous actresses which have played the part and in order to give a balance to the malevolence of the Villain, ten 'Good Fairies' will be discussed.

Descending from the ceiling of the Liverpool Empire on a wire high above the stage and dressed in a golden sparkly gown to rapturous audience applause, it could only be the wonderful **Cilla Black** (1943-2015). Born in Liverpool she harboured strong ambitions to be a singer. Cilla began her show business career as a singer and was championed by her friends 'The Beatles' who wrote many of the songs she recorded throughout her career.

She had eleven top ten hits in the British charts in the 1960s and the 1970s but also hosted her own variety show on BBC television between 1968 and 1976. Cilla's television career then evolved into becoming a prominent presenter, hosting television shows such as 'Blind Date' and 'Surprise, Surprise'. She became a regular fixture of Saturday night viewing.

But Cilla has been an influential figure in Pantomime. She made her first appearance as 'Little Red Riding Hood' at the Wimbledon Theatre in 1965. This was significant as she was partly responsible for reversing the trend of men being cast as Principal Boys, which had become the norm through the 1950s. Cilla starred again as Principal Boy in 'Aladdin' and made several forays into the role there after.

However with the maturation of years and a break from the annual Christmas show for several seasons, Cilla returned to triumphant acclaim at the Liverpool Empire, in 2008, as the Fairy Godmother. In many ways this was a magnificent home-coming for the 'Queen of Saturday Night' television; as she was surrounded by several local performers who had gone on to forge successful television careers such as Les Dennis and Jennifer Ellison.

After a successful career as a model in the 1980s and 1990s, **Linda Lusardi** has expanded her show business career to include television, film and stage appearances. On stage she has appeared in 'Pygmalion', 'Funny Peculiar' and 'Not Now Darling' as well as countless other productions. Her television parts include long standing roles in the ITV series 'Emmerdale' and 'The Bill'. But she has also presented on the show 'Loose Women'.

Pantomime has been central to her transition away from her modelling career and into the broader world of entertainment. She first starred in Pantomime in 1988 and usually stars with her husband, Sam Kane, in the annual Christmas show. Indeed the show business life is very much a family affair with her two children pursuing their own theatrical careers.

During this time she has switched roles from being the Principal Girl in 'Snow White' to the Wicked Queen and the Fairy Godmother in 'Cinderella'. She enjoys the family atmosphere of the Pantomime and although she had no formal theatrical training, she has undergone a steep learning curve to learn on the job with a series of supportive fellow actors and directors. Her versatility is demonstrated by her capacity to take on new challenges such as 'Dancing on Ice' and 'Come Dine with Me'. As well as her show business career Linda is also a successful businesswoman with a range of interests including cosmetics and writing.

Best known for her role as Tracey Stubbs in the television situation comedy 'Birds of a Feather', **Linda Robson** has been a regular Pantomime performer for several years. Born in Islington, London, she attended the Anna Scher Theatre School and went on to star in a number of television shows either as an actress, presenter or reality television shows such as 'I'm a Celebrity, Get Me Out of Here' and 'Celebrity Masterchef'. She almost fell into acting as a youngster when she was introduced to a teacher, Anna Scher, who ran acting classes for children at 10p a class. Soon the class was attracting the interest of casting directors who were drawn to the working class children and their enthusiasm and authenticity. The school produced a plethora of well-known actors and actresses.

After a hesitant television start, she was reunited with her school pal, Pauline Quirke, and the actress Lesley Joseph in 'Birds of a Feather' which became the highest rated comedy series on BBC TV. Blessed with a strong London accent, Linda uses her cockney drawl to good effect in her stage work. She enjoys the Pantomime experience because of the camaraderie of the cast and the way in which the cast becomes an extended family at this time of year, particularly when you are likely to be away from your own family during the Christmas season.

There was a time when **Wendy Craig** had the monopoly in playing the scatty, middle-aged housewife on British television. She was so good at the art of playing the part that she was in danger was getting shoe-horned into such parts for all of her career. But Wendy is too talented and versatile an actress, to allow this situation to happen. Indeed before her prominent television roles in such shows as 'Not in Front of the Children' and 'Butterflies', she enjoyed a strong career in films and on stage, where she has made several West End performances.

Born in the North-East in Durham, she developed a keen interest in acting at school after being cast as the lead in a large number of school productions. Wendy trained at the Central School of Dramatic Art and graduated to appearances on stage and screen. But it was her roles in the role of the bewildered housewife and mother on the television in the late 1960s and 1970s which made her a household name. Furthermore she developed her writing career with series such as 'Nanny' and 'Laura and Disorder', in which she starred in as well.

Her Pantomime appearances are legendary. Wendy has extensive Pantomime experience and has become a regular performer on the Christmas stage. She brings a majestic quality to the role of the benevolent Fairy and has waved her wand in several shows around the provinces. It is her maturity, experience and star quality which make her a much sought after cast member for the Pantomime season.

Despite being one of the most photographed and talked about celebrities in the 1970s and 1980s, **Britt Ekland**, is never happier than being on stage at the Pantomime playing the part of the Fairy Godmother. Born in Stockholm, Sweden Britt found her way to England in the 1960s and soon started to make her name in television, stage and film. She starred as the Bond girl, Mary Goodnight, in 'The Man with the Golden Gun' in 1974 and in such celebrated films such as 'Get Carter' and 'Wicker Man'. In total she starred in over 30 films alongside such leading men such as Michael Caine, Roger Moore, Peter Sellars and Yul Brynner.

She first played Pantomime in 1992 and has been a regular performer ever since. She is attracted by the glamour and the bright lights of the show and also the ability to manipulate the script and ad lib lines as well as being able to develop a rapport with the audience. As the Fairy Godmother she has starred alongside Bradley Walsh and Danny La Rue. Coming from Sweden she admits that Pantomime could only work in the UK as the audiences have grown up with the eccentric scripts and bizarre characters.

Although she has reached a grand age, Britt retains her glamorous looks and enjoys the interaction with the audience and the references made to previous events in her life, some of which are aimed more at the mums and dads in the audience than the children. She is also able to take her beloved dog along to the shows knowing that when she is on stage, other members of the cast will look after the dog because the show is, to her, like being in an extended family.

Although only making her Pantomime debut in 2015, **Dillie Keane** is set to be one of the stars of the future in Pantoland. Born in Ireland and with a strong musical training, she studied acting at the London Academy of Music and Dramatic Art before finding her way into cabaret as one third of the comedy trio 'Fascinating Aida'.

The trio have played five West End seasons, released five albums and published two books and DVDs. They are regular performers in Cabaret or on stage when they tour the country. Although the membership of the group has changed over the years, Dillie has been one of the constant performers in the trio.

But Dillie has a very strong and prominent solo career as an actress, comedienne, song-writer and broadcaster. She has been nominated twice, once with Fascinating Aida and once as a solo artist, for the prestigious Perrier Award at the Edinburgh Festival and won the Best Comedy Award at the Moers Comedy Festival in 2001.

Her versatility makes her a well sought after performer who is often touring with the comedy trio or in her one woman shows. In 2015 she appeared at the Yvonne Arnaud Theatre in Guildford in her first Pantomime 'Jack and the Beanstalk' and went down a storm with her singing, dancing and acting prowess.

Now known mainly for her appearances as a judge on the television talent show 'Britain's Got Talent', **Amanda Holden**, has a career which includes several Pantomime appearances. Born in Portsmouth she showed her abilities at school and as a member of the Bishop's Waltham Little Theatre Company. When she left school Amanda trained at the Mountview Theatre School in Wood Green, London.

It was not long before she was making a name for herself

on stage and television and her early Pantomime career was in conjunction with her then husband, the comedian and actor Les Dennis. However her solo career progressed and she starred in the ITV television series 'Wild at Heart' for three seasons as well as the television comedies 'Kiss Me Kate' and The Grimleys'. On stage Amanda won acclaim for the title role 'Thoroughly Modern Millie' for which she won the Laurence Olivier Theatre Award in 2004. She was also Princess Fiona in the original West End production of 'Shrek the Musical'. Understandably with such a busy schedule she found it hard to commit to a regular Pantomime season particularly as motherhood was an important consideration.

However it has recently been announced that Amanda will be returning to the Pantomime stage and will appear as the Fairy Godmother in the 2016 London Palladium production of 'Cinderella'. This will be the first time the theatre has hosted a Pantomime since 1987. The production has an all-star cast and is scheduled to run for a limited five week season.

One of the greatest actresses of the British stage and screen, **Dame Anna Neagle**, (1904-1986) made a belated entrance as a Fairy Godmother in the 1970s and 1980s. Born Florence Robertson she became one of the most successful box-office draws in Post-War Britain in a series of comedies and historical dramas which lifted the spirits of the population after the troubles and tribulations of war time austerity and suffering. Anna was known for bringing glamour and sophistication to her roles as well as being a versatile actress who could sing, dance and act.

She made her stage debut in 1917 as a dancer and by 1931 she was starring as the lead actress in the West End musical 'Stand Up and Sing' with Jack Buchanan. In the audience was the film director, Herbert Wilcox, who had come to see Buchanan with a view to casting him in films. Wilcox was so impressed with Neagle that he encouraged her to pursue a film career under his direction. Forming an alliance with Wilcox, who was later to become her husband, she went on to star in a number of classic films and portrayed a number of female historical figures in films such as; 'Nell Gwynn', 'Victoria the Great' and 'Nurse Edith Cavell'. Anna sought to retire in 1957 after her last film 'The Lady in the Square'.

But her husband was declared bankrupt in 1964 and she was forced to return to the stage and appeared in a succession of West End productions before embarking on a belated Pantomime career. She played the Fairy Godmother at the Alexandra Theatre, Birmingham in 1974 and continued to play the role up until her appearance at the London Palladium in 1985, a year before her death in 1986.

Malandra Burrows was born in Woolton, Liverpool and was encouraged by her mother to begin dancing at an early age. As a result she appeared in Yorkshire Television's 'Junior Showtime' at the age of six. Subsequently she became the youngest ever winner of the Television Talent Show 'New Faces' at the grand old age of nine.

Malandra joined the Everyman Youth Theatre in Liverpool and did classes at the Liverpool Theatre School whilst honing her skills in amateur productions and carrying on with her school work. When she left school Malandra enrolled at a Liverpool drama school and spent two years finely tuning her craft and developing her all round skills of singing, acting and dancing.

Shortly after leaving drama school she auditioned for the part of Kathy Bates in the popular television soap opera 'Emmerdale' and got the part. She became one of the longest serving characters in the show appearing in the soap opera from 1985 to 2001 but making guest appearances on special occasions. The character is best remembered for being one of the most married women in the show and having a reputation for having the 'kiss of death' on her male partners.

Since leaving 'Emmerdale' Malandra has enjoyed a very successful career as the Fairy Godmother in a succession of Pantomime productions in provincial theatres across the UK. Her glamour and versatility as a performer make her a natural for the part and she has appeared with many of the classic Pantomime performers on stage to the delight of the many fans of 'Emmerdale'.

One of the biggest television stars of the 1970s and 1980s, **Linda Gray**, made the transition into Pantomime at a mature age but showed that she had what it takes to be a glamourous and magical Fairy Godmother in the 2014 production of 'Cinderella' at the Wimbledon Theatre.

She sprang to fame as the long-suffering wife of the devious oil baron J. R. Ewing in the CBS television series 'Dallas'. Born in California, she started her career as a model appearing in numerous television commercials. In fact the legs portrayed on the poster of the Oscar winning film 'The Graduate' do not belong to the film's female lead, Anne Bancroft, but to Linda Gray!

Whilst modelling, Linda made several appearances in feature films and television and made the transition to television. But it was 'Dallas' which brought her to the public's consciousness. She made regular appearances in the series between 1978 and 1989 and featured in many of the numerous spin-offs which followed. The programme certainly stretched her acting credentials with corruption, betrayal, greed, lies, affairs and evil being part of the everyday happenings at the Southfork Ranch, where she lived at with J. R.

When she agreed to play the role of the Fairy Godmother in London, Linda had never been exposed to this traditional genre of theatre. She was worried that she might be thrown by the audiences calling out her television name and become distracted. But like a true professional she added a little bit of US sparkle to the Christmas show and delighted audiences with her wand waving abilities, Texas style!

Chapter Seven
The Etiquette of Pantomime

It has already been suggested that the Pantomime story is basically a battle of 'Good' against 'Evil'. No matter if the story is set in medieval England, ancient China, exotic Egypt or fantasy land, the overall moral of the story is that 'Good' will triumph over 'Evil'. However in order to reach the outcome which the Pantomime requires there are a stock list of characters who play out the story and are either on the side of 'good' or 'evil'. Their names, occupations, social backgrounds and social classes might change but the essential intention of the character stays the same.

It is important to understand that each character has a particularly role to play in their interaction with the audience. So the audience needs to know how to react to each character in order to get the most out of the Pantomime experience. The hero or protagonist is usually a young man but can be a young woman in the case of Pantomimes such as 'Cinderella'. They are good hearted but poor and are caught up in extraordinary or magical events. When they are on stage, they need to be cheered loudly particularly in any conflict or stage fight scene. They need to be cheered doubly with the most resounding shouts of approval when they finally defeat the Villain.

The Villain who is portrayed as evil as possible, by contrast, should be booed and hissed with as much enthusiasm as the hero is cheered. But do not stop there as his or her henchmen can be subject to the same levels of disapproval as the Villain. The evil person will be condescending and patronising towards the audience and will consider themselves the superior of those whom he or she interacts with. They need to be treated with distain every time they enter and exit the stage and when they outline their devious plans to take over the world. However in the end they need to be treated with forgiveness and kindness and given the benefit of doubt when they express contrition and remorse.

Each protagonist will have a love interest. The love interest may be male or female but whatever their gender, they will be pure and of good heart just like the person who they are in love with. The love interest will find the protagonist funny and highly attractive. Even though the protagonist and the love interest are of the same gender, which happens with Principal boys and Principal Girls, the audience will be accepting of their love unconditionally.

There is always a Clown or Buffoon to provide the comic relief. They will be good-hearted and often display unrequited love for the protagonist love interest but will be too shy to challenge the protagonists or to admit his feelings for the love interest. The Buffoon will play on his shyness and reserved nature for part of the time with the audience but at other times they may appear confident. Usually they have a task of looking after an object or an animal and they will ask the audience to help them with this task often by getting to signal them when the object or animal is under threat. The audience should respond vigorously in their help with lots of shouting and encouragement. One other thing the Buffoon might be a bit simple so sometimes the audience must try to keep them informed of what is happening in the story or help them with their decision-making skills.

The Good Fairy embodies all that is righteous and watches over our hero. She will appear fleetingly and may act as a narrator. She will stand to the right or centre of the stage and will need to be listened to as her conversation may be conveyed in coupling rhymes. The Good Fairy deserves our attention as she can use her magical powers to rescue the hero and help 'Good' triumph over 'Evil'.

Perhaps the most recognisable character in the Pantomime is the Dame. She will come across as likeable, warm-hearted, unattractive and often slow-witted. The Dame will dress flamboyantly and the audience will need to appreciate the dress sense of the Dame, even though it may appear ridiculous. The costumes should be greeted with lots of 'oohhs' and 'aahhs' and sometimes with applause. The Dame will talk to the audience and express how impoverished she is in life. She has no money and no man to love her. The audience will need to be over-sympatric to her telling of her woes. Much of the Dame character's humour stems from her efforts to maintain appearances of ladylike dignity. This is despite being naturally graceless and coarse and whilst getting into undignified and often ludicrous situations. Be kind to the Dame, she deserves to be loved!

Most Pantomimes have an animal part. It may be big like Dick Whittington's cat or relatively minor to the plot such as a Pantomime horse. The animal is always endearing unless employed by the Villain. It will appeal to children and will be soft hearted. The costume will be outlandish and brightly coloured and often adorned with spotty patterns or shaggy fringes. The animal will be great fun and usually will not be able to talk, apart from Puss in Boots. So its gestures will be exaggerated and appear comic when performed. Like any domestic animal it needs to be cared for.

As well as responding to different ways to the characters, there are a number of conventions, some of which have weakened or changed over the course of the years but which add to the enjoyment of the performance. For example the use of risqué double entendre, often wringing innuendo out of a perfectly innocent phrase, may be employed by some characters particularly the Dame or one of her potential suitors.

A double entendre is a figure of speech or a particular way of wording that is devised to be understood in either of two ways, having a double meaning. Typically one of the meanings is obvious, given the context whereas the other may require more thought. The innuendo may convey a message that could be socially awkward, sexually suggestive or offensive to state directly. The double entendre may exploit puns to convey the second meaning and therefore exploit the ambiguity of what is being said. In Pantomime the double entendre means that things can be said which have one meaning for adults and one meaning for children.

The music may be original but is more likely to combine well-known tunes with lyrics which have been re-written to reflect the content or locality of the Pantomime. There may well be one or more audience participation song. It is traditional to sing the song in different ways such as getting one half of the audience singing one verse and another part singing a separate verse in a competitive way. Alternatively all the men in the audience might have to sing one part and the females another verse. The traditional song will usually be led by the Dame with the help of others.

The Good Fairy will always enter the stage from the right (the audience's left) and the Villain from stage left (or the audience's right). This reflects the medieval belief that heaven is on the right and the left side symbolised hell. At some point during the show the Dame and the Buffoon might sit on a bench and sing a cheerful song to forget their fears. The thing they fear will appear on the stage behind them but at first the characters will ignore the audience's warnings and carry on singing. The traditional call of 'It's behind you' will need to be shouted louder and louder in order to alert the characters of the danger they may face. The scene will generally end with one or more of the characters encountering the fearful thing, screaming and running off the stage being chased by their fear!

Slapstick is an essential part of most shows with a designated slapstick scene such as baking or cooking. It can get messy on stage but the carnage rarely spills out from the stage so the audience are safe from the spillage which ensues. Occasionally some water or flour might escape but this can be brushed off most items of clothing!

An essential part of any Pantomime is the chorus who are the extras on stage. They often appear in multiple scenes and will perform a variety of singing, dancing and acting parts to add to the story. All members of the cast will expect applause at the end of the show in the traditional walk down. This usually proceeds with the junior members of the cast first and then the lead characters last with the hero and their beau the last to walk down and receive the audience's appreciation.

Now we have reached the end of the show with the walk down it is a good point to close the book. Here's hoping you have learned a little bit more about the traditional theatrical experience known as the Pantomime and that your Pantomime experience will be enhanced by what you have read. Enjoy the performance, join in with the show and laugh as loudly as you want to!

Printed in Great Britain
by Amazon

54294757R00059